Living at the Crossroads

Wendy Aridela

Copyright © 2013 Wendy Aridela
All rights reserved.
ISBN: 13: 978-1490924045

CONTENTS

Acknowledgements	5
Note on terminology	6
The Prologue	7
Chapter 1: Choices	10
Chapter 2: Why Change?	14
Chapter 3: Noticing the Choices	23
Chapter 4: What do you Want?	28
Chapter 5: Who Wants It?	47
Chapter 6: Are You Shining?	60
Chapter 7: Changing the World	76
Chapter 8: Begin Now!	84
Chapter 9: Meditation	96
Chapter 10: Being Authentic	106
Chapter 11: Things that go Bump	120
Chapter 12: Life as Co-Conspirator	135
Chapter 13: Living in the Now	151
Chapter 14: Living at the Crossroads	167
Chapter 15: Some Final Thoughts	188

ACKNOWLEDGEMENTS

With deepest thanks to all the people who believed in me:
Elanor, Mack, Ruth and Kath most of all, but also Harriet, Jacqui, Jayne, Caroline, Sue, Jill, Lisa, Estelle, and Sarah - I'd never have done it without you!

NOTE ON TERMINOLOGY

In any book on a Spiritual topic, there's the vexed question of what to call "it" - the great and wonderful energy behind everything.
God? Universe? Spirit? Basic Goodness? I've used all of these terms interchangeably - and maybe several others.
If any of them grates on you, apologies. Please feel free at any point to mentally translate the term I am using for one you feel more comfortable with.

THE PROLOGUE

All of the worry, doubt and restlessness fell away as the silence within became deeper and deeper. I could feel myself dropping into intense stillness. This was turning into a very deep and centred experience of meditation, much stronger than usual. Suddenly a brilliant point of light appeared in my inner field of vision. More points of light started emerging until I was held in a vast sea of brilliance which washed through me, soaking every cell of my body with love and grace.

Then the radiance began to take shape before my inner eye, forming a vast, complex Mandala of unbelievable beauty. As the stillness grew even more profound, I found myself surrounded by an immense pattern of light which I knew was the "back stage view" of the whole of Creation.

From the normal everyday world Creation looks like trees and clouds, people of every kind, wild animals, and flowers - the whole visible environment. From here, we see suffering, ugliness, greed, pollution and problems. But from there it's all brilliant light, woven together in a way that is perfectly beautiful and harmonious.

Each separate strand of light represented a life, woven in with the other strands to make a design I couldn't hold in my mind afterwards but that I thought had been a bit like a Turkish carpet. (Although about 5 dimensional, and much more complex - but in a way that slid off my 3-D mind when I tried to remember it in normal consciousness.)

In our everyday lives, we seem to encounter dead-ends. We meet circumstances where we are suddenly steered off in a totally different direction and places where we have to back-track - often, it seems, for no reason at all. Just another of life's snarl-ups. Just bad luck. Just life being the typical mess that it so often turns out to be. But from there, all the zigzags and the U-turns are part of the pattern. From there, the whole thing makes total sense.

From there, something else was also apparent - some people's lives were shining much more than the others. Some people's light-strands were flickering on and off like faulty neon tubes. Other strands shone with a dim glow. Some twinkled and sparkled. Yet there were some that shone brilliantly, lighting up other strands whose paths they crossed and illuminating their bit of the Mandala - making the whole thing more beautiful.

I could clearly see that the Mandala was intended to have all the strands lit up. If every strand lit up, the Mandala would be completed, its loveliness perfected. What seemed to make the difference in whether someone's strand was illumined was how "on track" they were living.

I knew that from then on I would do everything I could to light up myself and all the people around me. Just the idea of making that Mandala even a tiny bit more beautiful brought tears to my eyes. I committed myself to the task from the depths of my heart.

I had absolutely no idea how to do it.
It's taken me over 25 years to find out.
This book is the result.

CHAPTER 1: CHOICES

Where are you now?

Where are you now? There's obviously a sensible answer you could make to that - I'm in the kitchen, I'm at the office, I'm on the bus, I'm at the coffee shop. But whether you know it or not, right now you are at a crossroads. This is always true - it's not that there is something particularly special about now, compared with every other moment in your life. At this very moment, dozens of paths fan out from where you are. Starting now, your life could go off in many different directions.

It may only take a tiny shift in the next few weeks, over the next few days, even in the next five minutes, to make the difference between whatever you have now and a much richer life - one filled with joy, love, and a powerful sense of really making a difference in the world.

This isn't a goal-setting book. It's not a book about how you can magnetise all kinds of good things towards you so that you can have an amazing future, full of fast cars, jewellery, a big house and life in the fast lane.

It's a book about having a richer _now_. It's a book about discovering who you _really_ are, and discovering why you were born - what you chose to come here to contribute to the world. It's a book about living "on purpose."

To quote Jack Canfield, world-famous author of the "Chicken Soup for the Soul" books:

> "Everyone has a Gift to give.
> It's the essence of who they are."

Finding and developing your Gift is a journey of discovery that has no end - because it's always happening now.

You've no doubt heard the idea that most of us only use 1% of our brains. Scientifically, I don't think that's true - it comes from the days when researchers didn't have all the wonderful brain-scanners that exist these days and so they had no way to find out what most of the brain was doing at any moment. If the only way you are able to find out about what brains do is to wait until their owners are dead and then slice up the brain and look at it under a microscope, it's hardly surprising that you may come to the conclusion that most of it isn't doing much!

Now we have modern brain scanners, it's apparent that most of us are using a large part of our brain a lot of the time.

However, it's indisputably true that most of us are only using a tiny percentage of our Gift. No matter how much of it you uncover, there is always more. Discovering "the essence of who you are" is the work of a life-time - the most amazing and rewarding work any of us can ever do.

So this is a book about discovering and developing your Gift. This is not some toy-filled future that you are going to have to magnetise towards you. It's not a promotion or a qualification you are going to have to work like a Trojan for the next five years to achieve. You already have your Gift - it's within you right now. Uncovering it, and living in ways that increasingly express it, will be the most wonderful adventure you have ever set out on. It's like discovering, after months or years of struggling to make ends meet, that there is buried treasure in your cellar.

Your journey can start now. This is one of those crossroads I was talking about. Right now, your life can change - or not. You can put this book down and say <u>no</u> to all the ideas in it.

You may feel intrigued, but put it down to look at later. Perhaps in a few days, when you're not so busy or so stressed. Maybe in a few weeks. Or a few months. Or perhaps a few years?

Ask yourself an honest question - how has indefinitely putting off stuff worked for you in the past? My experience is that tomorrow never comes! If I put off stuff for long enough - and that's sometimes not very long- I forget about it entirely.
So will you join me now?
Say <u>yes</u> here and your journey can begin today!

Getting A "Round Toowit"
I remember once seeing a shop which sold little circular metal plaques, inscribed with the words "A Round Toowit" The writing on the box said: "You know all those things you were going to get done when you got "a Round Toowit?" Well, you've got one now - so get on with them!"
Don't wait until someone finds "a Round Toowit" and gives <u>you</u> one. Make a decision to start the journey now. Please. You deserve it.

CHAPTER 2: WHY CHANGE?

So, you decided to take the next step - fantastic! Let's talk a bit more about the crossroads.

How come I don't see the choices?

It's easy to understand the idea of having different paths fanning out from each moment, depending on the direction of our next step. It's harder to see the choices in each moment. Our brain is hard-wired to get as much of our lives as possible running on automatic, with little or no conscious thought. That's obviously a very efficient way to do things.

I could drive from here to Manchester while listening to the radio in my car, carrying on a conversation with my passengers, mentally having a row with my boss or my best-beloved (which I'd win, of course!) or planning out the next chapter of this book. I'd only have to totally focus on the driving if I got into slow-moving traffic, or encountered hazardous conditions like pouring rain or fog that reduced my visibility. We all do the same, running whole chunks of our lives on automatic pilot. However, that does mean that most of the time we do most of the same things, with predictably the same results. We eat the same things for breakfast most days. We drive the same way to work.

If we go out, we visit the same places and the same people. We read the same magazines or newspapers. We watch the same TV programs. Unconsciously, we tend to repeat the same decisions - so much so, that much of the time, we're not even aware of having made a decision at all.

It's as if we're wearing blinkers, so that at every crossroads, we only see the direction that is straight ahead. So we get more of the same. I'd like to invite you to take off the blinkers, and to make more conscious choices. A small change in the next five minutes could mean that, one year from now, you're in a very different place than you would have been.

I read that when Concorde - the supersonic plane that used to take passengers from London to New York - was flying, it went so fast that the pilots couldn't help but be slightly off course more than 90% of the time. It was like flying in zigzags - constant course-corrections. They knew that being just one or two degrees off course could mean that they'd end up over Boston, or Greenland, instead of New York. In the same way, changing your life now by just 1% or 2% - a change you may barely notice - can make a big difference to where you end up.

Big Choice? Small Choice?

Clearly, there could be some paths in every moment that would bring enormous changes into your life very quickly. You could step in front of a speeding truck and be disabled - or even killed. You could meet the love of your life. You could buy a winning lottery ticket. But most changes are much smaller, and the results are harder to see immediately. For example, you get massively overweight one little cookie at a time. One cookie makes no apparent difference at all. However, over twenty or more years of cookie-eating, the effect is huge.

Even when you are aware that there are choices to be made, you are much likelier to make some choices than others. Again this isn't necessarily a bad thing - you probably don't <u>want</u> to become a heroin addict, so you would dismiss that choice instantly, if it ever crossed your path. Similarly, unless there was some incredibly fabulous reason for it, you're unlikely to just uproot yourself and go and live in Antarctica next week, or the Kalahari desert. You possibly <u>could</u> do these things, but you wouldn't because there's no reason in your life right now to go and do them.

But you may be missing some choices simply because it doesn't cross your mind that they exist. For example, some people wouldn't even consider going to University when they leave school because "Our family aren't that kind of people; we don't go to University." There's maybe nothing stopping you - you might even have passed all the necessary exams or be able to take them in evening classes at a local college - but it has honestly never occurred to you that getting a degree could be a real possibility. So you might immediately delete all the possibilities for your life that involve getting qualifications at that level.

You may be afraid of making some kinds of choices because of bad experiences in your past. For example, if you've just come out of a very hurtful relationship, it can sometimes be months or even years before you feel able to relax again and trust in love. Even if you meet someone who seems interested in you, you may mentally delete all the choices that involve getting into a relationship with them, for fear of getting seriously hurt.

On another level, we refer to some changes that some people go through as "miraculous." A person visits a healer or goes to a holy place on a pilgrimage and is suddenly cured of a disease that everybody expected would be fatal.

Or someone who has been trying unsuccessfully for years to have a baby adopts a child and then discovers that they are pregnant. Or an alcoholic who has battled drink for half a lifetime finds God and walks away from the booze forever.

It seems that, at some points in life, some people are able to totally rewrite the script, and to start living from a completely different story. Their whole identity undergoes a shift. How do those kinds of changes happen? Is there any way to <u>make</u> them happen - or even to make them more likely? How can we open to miracles?

Even when we're aware that we have choices right now, how do we get to recognise what is available to us? And how do we know which choices will lead to the best outcomes for our lives? We've all experienced making mistakes - thinking that this is our dream job or our true love - and then being bitterly disappointed. So how can we recognise sooner when a choice <u>is</u> going wrong? When the "dream job" turns out to include workmates from Hell? Or our "true love" is starting to look suspiciously like an addict? One key learning is that we are always at the crossroads. You can't choose once and then be done with it for the rest of your life, any more than you could take a bath once and stay clean forever.

Even if you manage to keep your life largely unchanging for a long period of time, circumstances will often come and get you, dragging you into change willy-nilly, whether you want to change or not.

Getting your arm twisted

Life has a habit of twisting your arm when it's time for you to change. The first indicators are usually fairly quiet. You start to feel unfulfilled at work. You have some doubts about your relationship. You have some odd dreams. Some people pick up the cues at this point. They start rewriting their CV/resume, they schedule a review with their Manager, they have a long talk to their nearest and dearest and they start to consider their options.

Other people resolutely close their eyes and ears and continue "business as normal." What tends to happen then is that life hints more loudly. You get a whole load of grunt work dumped on you. There's lipstick on his collar. You start to get sick from the stress. The new boss turns out to be a minion of the Dark Side. The weird dreams become regular nightmares that wake you gasping and covered in sweat. At this point, many more people get the message and start to make some changes.

Even then, some people still resolutely hang on in there. They may start muttering about looking for another job, but instead, they just adapt their life around the new 80-hour week and soldier on. They get prescription medicine to turn down the symptoms and stop their body's unhappiness getting in the way. They moan to their friends about how their partner is always working late, but leave it at that.

Finally, life starts shouting. You get made redundant or you get reassigned to the office in the Hebrides. You get fired. That stress you've been pushing down erupts into something serious that you can't possibly ignore. You come home one night to a note on the fridge. You get mugged, or wind up in a car crash. You have a breakdown. Three of your close friends die suddenly over a period of weeks and it feels as if it may be you next. Or you have a spiritual encounter that changes your life. You find God. You open your door to an angel. It may take a near-death experience, but at this point, most people do get it. They acknowledge that they have to change.

Other people feel equally pulled or pushed into change, but the process seems to come from somewhere deep inside rather than being driven by circumstances in the external world.

There may be a sense of calling that lasts for months or years and won't go away. There's a nagging feeling that you're meant to be doing something about world starvation, or dyslexic children or the destruction of natural ecosystems. You keep dreaming about performing your music, writing that book, exhibiting your art, or dancing as a way of life.

Of course, these are ridiculous day-dreams, you tell yourself. There's no way they can happen. You're not good enough. You're not qualified. You have no money. You have eight kids to support. You don't know anybody influential. You live in a tiny village in the middle of nowhere. You're no-one special. You're just ordinary. But not only do the day-dreams refuse to go away, they get stronger.

You keep having vivid dreams that seem to have a message. You see the same sequence of numbers everywhere you go. You keep having conversations with people that somehow end up being about your dream. There's the waitress who tells you about her dyslexic nephew who's having such trouble at school. The person at the station who tells you about their volunteer work in India. The lady in the checkout line who mistakes you for that famous singer. Life seems to be <u>nagging</u> you.

Or you may be one of those people who just wake up one morning to a feeling they have somehow crossed a line and the world is now different. You feel you've grown out of life, in some indefinable way. Up until yesterday, you loved your work; now, it seems meaningless, unchallenging, unrewarding. You don't know what to do instead but you know you must do something different, and as soon as possible, or die inside. Your relationship has been quietly chugging along for years in a comfortable routine; now, you see it as having been dead in the water for a long time and know it's time to move on. This kind of call to change can be devastating because it seems to come from nowhere. One day life is fine and the next day everything swirls into fog and dissolves.

So, one way or another, change enters your life. If a crisis erupts, you have to change. It gets forced upon you. What's more, following a crisis, you may have very few choices open to you. It may be impossible to avoid all crises, but it is possible to minimize their impact or to deflect them by being more aware of the choices in each moment and by making more conscious decisions about where you want to go next.

CHAPTER 3: NOTICING THE CHOICES

The Importance of Mindfulness

A key learning is that you can't make any choices at all unless you are aware of having a choice. Remember the automatic pilot I talked about earlier? Well, this is one of the ways in which it is a liability rather than an asset. While you are zipping through your day on your "repeat yesterday" setting, all kinds of opportunities may pass you by, simply because you aren't noticing anything much at the time.

If you're not aware of having any choices to make, you won't make any. Your whole life will tend to continue in a straight line, with "more of the same" happening over and over. It's as simple as that. So one of the things I'll be talking about is paying attention in the moment to what is going on - some people refer to this as Mindfulness.

The more you practice mindfulness, the richer your experience of life will become. You'll notice the little flowers growing in the cracks in the pavement/sidewalk and the sounds of the birds behind the traffic noise.

You'll notice the smells - the wonderful cinnamon smell as you pass a bakery, the smell of the new-mown grass in the park, the way that the smell of the street changes after it's rained.

Most importantly, you'll start to be aware that you could choose differently - <u>now</u> and <u>now</u> and <u>now</u>. You have just a split second before you lose your temper to take a deep breath and to walk away. You have a moment before that cookie touches your lips to change your mind and to put it down. In a conversation or a negotiation you start to say "yes" and then realise you could say "no". Or someone presents an opportunity to you and you start to say "no" and then - in that tiny gap of paying attention - you think "Well, why not?"?
To give you a taste of mindfulness, here's a simple experiment to try:

WHOLE-HEARTED DOING
This is one of the simplest mindfulness practices of all, but it's wonderfully practical. A good time to practice is next time you make a hot drink.

1. When you've read through these instructions, go and make yourself a hot drink.

2. You can have any drink you want, so before you make your usual "instant-coffee-with-a-splash-of-milk-and-two-sugars," take a minute to tune into your body. Right now, is that what you most feel like drinking? Imagine some alternatives, to give yourself a choice. What would it be like to a have a cup of tomato soup now? Or some cocoa with a sprinkle of cinnamon? Or lemon and honey? Or a cup of tea? You may still decide on your old favourite but at least now it is a real choice.

3. Once you've decided on a drink, make it. But pay total attention to what you're doing. If you notice your mind has wandered off into gas-bill territory, bring it back to the present. Notice the weight of the kettle and how it changes as you add water. Listen to the sound as the water comes to the boil. Feel the textures of the cup, the spoon, the milk carton. See all the colours around you with new eyes. Smell the coffee/cocoa/soup/tea. Become aware of the background sounds, including the ones in the distance. Keep your mind on what is really here, rather than talking to yourself about it.

4. When you've made the drink, drink it. Focus on the tastes and feelings. Keep your attention on the experience of drinking. Savour each sip – as if this was your last cuppa on earth.

5. Clean up, noticing what you are doing, and the sounds, colours and textures around you.

How was that? How different was it from previous experiences of making a drink? How well were you able to keep your mind on the task?
If you do this for a week, every time you make a drink, what do you notice? Does it get easier? Or do you get more skilled at noticing your mental rambling so that it actually seems to get harder? (This isn't a trick question – there isn't a 'right' answer!)
You can do this with any task - washing up, changing the baby's nappy/diaper, cutting the grass - whatever.

If you enjoyed experimenting with Mindfulness, try this meditation that's also based on simply paying attention to stuff your automatic pilot would normally delete from your world.

MEDITATION PRACTICE: LISTENING TO THE SILENCE

Please take note - I love this meditation but I find it does change your state quite a lot. So don't do it when you're driving, operating machinery, looking after little kids, etc!

1. Get comfortable - sit, lie, recline, kneel, whatever.

2. You can either listen to music, or to the sounds of nature - great outside on a warm day! - or to ordinary background sounds like traffic, and street noises.

3. Just relax and listen. Keep listening for the most subtle sound you can hear.

4. Whenever you hear a quieter, more subtle sound in the background, focus on that.

5. Keep going as long as you like - this is really great, however long you do it, so long as you can stay focused.

6. If you keep going long enough, you may start to hear the vast, deep silence behind all the sounds. If you hear it, listen to it and go deeper. (If you don't, enjoy the sounds anyway!)

CHAPTER 4: WHAT DO YOU WANT?

Choosing a Better Now

So, now you're more aware of having choices, let's think about how you start using that awareness to choose a better now.

If I stopped you in the street and asked if you could give me some directions because I was lost, what would be the first question you'd ask? I'm sure it would be: "Well, where do you want to go?"

It's the same at the crossroads you face in each moment. Which is the right direction to take depends very much on where you want to end up. If you haven't a clue what kind of a life you want, it's going to be very hard to choose a path that leads to happiness and fulfilment.

This is exactly where most people are. Either they've never thought at all about what they want in life - assuming that they just had to make the best of whatever came along or trust to luck, or fate - or they unquestioningly accept the vision of the good life presented by the media.

You know what I mean - a life with a big house, a high-status car, designer clothes, a glamorous partner, a toned body, private schooling for your kids, a holiday villa next to a brilliant blue ocean and lots of diamond jewellery. But for each of us, the recipe for deep joy and total fulfilment in life is different. Before you set out to "Live The Dream" you need to be sure that it's <u>your</u> dream that you're setting out to live.

The Law of Attraction - is that what I need?

You may have seen books and videos about "The Law of Attraction." These say that by focusing on the things you want to be, do and have, you will magnetise them to you and they will turn up in your life. To a certain extent this seems to be true. You've probably read stories about celebrities who say they knew at 6 years old that they wanted to win an Olympic Gold medal or an Oscar. Or heard of dancers who decided the very first time they saw a ballet that, one day, it would be them up on the stage, dancing like that. Or you've come across sportsmen who tell how Uncle Fred took them to a football match when they were 7 years old and they had a vision implanted in their mind that one day, they would be the goalkeeper for England.

As you read their story in a magazine, long after it's all come true, it's apparent that these guiding visions kept them going through thick and thin.

You'll have experienced this on a smaller scale for yourself at some point, I'm sure. There are days you get out of bed, dreading the day ahead, sure that everything will go wrong and - Ta-Da! - it all <u>does</u> go wrong. You have a total beast of a day, with almost non-stop disasters. On the other hand there are the occasions when you walk into a building for a job interview and just know that you're going to get the job and that you'll love working for these people. The picture in your head and the feeling in your bones turns into your lived reality, too. You <u>do</u> get the job and the people are fabulous to work for.

It really does seem to be the case that holding a clear picture of your desired outcome in your head, coupled with a strong emotion, tends to propel you towards making it happen - as long as you don't have hidden negative thoughts that keep sabotaging the process. And this is because the less verbal, less rational parts of your mind that hold images and work with emotion can't tell the difference between imagination and reality.

If you get a strong enough blueprint- a series of images linked with strong emotions - loaded into your imagination, you will have set yourself up to bring it about.

If you have any doubt about the power of your imagination to affect your concrete, physical reality, try the thought-experiment here.

WATCH YOUR SUBCONSCIOUS MIND IN ACTION!

Imagine it is a really hot day in Summer. The sun is shining from a cloudless blue sky. The lovely day has tempted you to go walking in the countryside, but it is so hot, you're beginning to wonder if this was such a good idea after all.

Even with sun-cream, your arms and face are feeling a bit sun-burnt and you're uncomfortably hot and sweaty. Worse still, the ground here is sandy and very dry, so as you walk, dust is getting kicked up. You can feel it sticking to your hot arms and legs and your mouth is starting to feel a bit gritty from where you've breathed it in. Your companion looks so dusty their clothes are grey with it in places, and you know you must look similar.

However, you know the view from the top of this next hill is going to be absolutely fantastic so you keep walking.

The path is steeper than you remembered, and it's hard work because of the loose sand and grit. Still, not much further now, you think - with some relief, because you can feel little trickles of perspiration sliding down your back. The dust is worse here than it was below and your mouth is feeling so dry. You promise yourself that as soon as you get to the top, you'll have a drink.

Finally - you made it! The view is amazing - it never fails to impress you. At the same time, you're ruefully aware that the back of your neck has definitely caught the sun - you can feel it smarting and your mouth is like sandpaper.

You get out your water bottle but before you take the long deep drink your body craves, your companion turns to you with a grin. "Try this" they say, - handing you a half a lemon, freshly sliced. The juice is dripping out of it and the sharp smell entices your nose. You bring the cool lemon up to your mouth and suck it, letting the refreshing acidity flood your mouth - WOW!
Now tell me - is your mouth watering?

When you imagine like this, your unconscious mind can't tell the difference between your imagination and reality. So it sends the same signals to your salivary glands as if you had <u>really</u> just sucked a lemon after a long, hot walk in the sun. Your imagination has a similar, very real effect on your life, just as it does on your body.

So, how does the Law of Attraction Work?

The basic premise of the Law of Attraction is that everything is energy, and has a characteristic frequency, including our thoughts and feelings. To attract something into your life, you magnetise it by matching frequencies with it. Your life will always tend to be an exact reflection of the frequencies that you are putting out. As, up until now, you have been doing this unconsciously, you have probably attracted quite a lot of negative events and people into your life, by emitting negative frequencies such as fear, doubt, worry and destructive criticism of yourself and others.

Once you realise that these negative thoughts and feelings attract the very negative events and people you have been worrying about, you can change what you are doing.

By holding positive thoughts and feelings, even when the outside world doesn't seem to be the way you'd like it to be, you begin to magnetise a different reality. As you feel more positive, cheerful and grateful, the circumstances of your life tend to improve.

To help them stay focused on their goals, people who are using the Law of attraction use a variety of tools.

Vision Boards

These are corkboards or sheets of card covered with photos, pictures, words and symbols that visually keep reminding you of your goal. For example, if you want a life-style that includes many foreign holidays, you may cut out photos from travel brochures, and print out the names of exotic places you'd like to visit, mounting them on a board with tickets, boarding passes, and souvenirs of past vacations. Every time you look at the board, it reminds you of your goal and helps to align you with it.

Affirmations

These are short phrases or sentences that you repeat many times over, to "reprogram" your unconscious mind.

So, for example, if you have a constant problem with cash-flow, you might say "Money now comes to me easily and quickly, from many unexpected sources." As you came to believe this on a deep level, your energy frequency would change and you could expect to find that, in fact, money <u>did</u> come in to you much more easily than before, and from many different directions.

Action

It's important to point out that usually, some kind of action will be required to effect the change. After all, if you keep on doing exactly what you have always done in the past, you are likely to get more of the same results you have been getting!

One of the main ways in which the Law of Attraction seems to work is that it opens your eyes to opportunities. Once you have decided what you want, and set a firm intention to get it, your subconscious mind starts looking for ways to bring that about. So you may get bright ideas out of the blue of actions to take, people to see, places to go, or products to develop.
You notice sources of information that may have always been there, but your automatic pilot was deleting your awareness of them because it didn't previously see that they were relevant to your life.

But now, you find books and websites that give you vital information, meet all kinds of useful people and discover organisations that are set up to help people in exactly your situation.

Using the Law of Attraction can be a valuable step in empowering yourself to make significant changes to your life. If you have never tried goal-setting before - especially if it had never before occurred to you that you had any kind of choice at all - then exploring the Law of Attraction can be a way of discovering for yourself how much your thoughts and feelings influence your life.

The downsides to setting goals

However, there are downsides to using goal-setting, especially if you try to stick rigidly to your plans. You can definitely overdo it! For a start, it tends to pull you out of being fully mindful right now into an imaginary future when you will be living a better life. The Law of Attraction process works best when you can feel in the present the feeling of having what you want in the future. But if you're focusing on feeling happy and grateful now primarily to get something better in the future, you're still being pulled away from the present.

The point of this is something you'll quickly realise once you start practising mindfulness. The only time you have is now - tomorrow is a fantasy and yesterday is just a memory. Even 5 minutes ago or 5 minutes into the future isn't really here - it's in your head. You're only here right now. Everything else exists in your imagination. It's not real.

Now there's nothing wrong with your imagination - it's a God-given gift. But it seems a bit of a waste of a real life, incarnated in a real body in the real world, to miss all of what is actually happening in favour of an imagined existence. Why bother incarnating? Right now is all the time you have to be happy, fulfilled and joyful. It seems a pity to miss it!

An over-reliance on goal-setting can lead to a type of tunnel-vision. You're so determined to achieve your dream exactly as you've imagined it that you can miss the magic in life. You miss the strange opportunities that can turn up when life goes off in its own direction, regardless of your plans. You miss all kinds of synchronicities and delightful surprises that appear along the way because you aren't aware of the here and now, only the future. You have your eye so firmly on the horizon that you miss the flowers at your feet.

The other disadvantage of goal-setting is that you are putting your happiness and fulfilment in something outside yourself. "I'll be happy when I finally have a Ferrari/ a Soul-Mate/ a scholarship to a prestigious college/ fill in the blank." Even if you're working on being happy now, your basic premise is that you'll be a whole lot <u>more</u> happy in the future when you've finally got the Ferrari or whatever.

The underlying belief behind "magnetising" things to you is that the stuff you want is out there. It's separate from you. You are not enough in yourself - you need this other thing to complete you. As long as you truly believe that happiness lies in getting - jobs, money, toys - you are unlikely to discover the deep joy that lies in becoming or in simply being.

You're also likely to discover, when you finally get all the stuff on your vision board, that in the long-term it doesn't make you as happy as you thought it would. Until you have a handle on who you are at a deeper level than everyday ho-hum reality and you start to get a feel for the true desires that are buried in the depths of your heart, you'll tend to go for the pre-packaged version of success that we're all sold every day via the media.

I've seen so many Vision boards that are almost identical! Yes, you may want a different kind of high-status car. Your friend wants a Mercedes, but you want a Lexus. The Caribbean beach-side villa you want may be in Barbados, while your friend's is on Saint Kitts but basically you've both bought the same package.

You've probably heard the quote:

> "You don't want to spend a lifetime climbing the ladder of Success, only to find, when you get to the top, that your ladder was leaning against the wrong wall!"

In the same way, you don't want to spend years creating a vision-board life for yourself, only to discover that you've materialised someone else's vision. This brings to mind a famous quote by the great artist, Michelangelo:

> " The greater danger for most of us is not that our aim is too high and we miss it - but that it is too low and we reach it. "

Many of us have no idea what we want at a deep level. Our society inspires us to achieve goals that are largely worthless in the long term.

There was a book that became a best-seller recently about how to make so much money that you'd only have to work a four-hour week. It made me sad to see it, because the person who wrote it - and probably most of the people who bought it - had so obviously never discovered the pure joy that comes from doing the work that makes your heart sing - work that doesn't even seem like "work" but more like a kind of deep play, work you would do for free, even if you won the Lottery.

You may gain status if you become a billionaire. It may give you a sense of security or an enduring pride in providing well for your family. But it won't give you that sense of living a deeply satisfying and worthwhile life that you'll get from discovering and developing your Gift. I'm not saying that there's anything wrong with being a billionaire. If you find a way to make living your Gift reap you billions, and that's what you want to do, fantastic!

But ultimately, you'll get the richest possible life - which may not be the life with the most cash - by living the life you were born for, by becoming the best version of who you really are.
So how on Earth do you find out who you really are and what you really want? I was hoping you'd ask that.

Finding out who you are

In the Western world, we live in a culture dominated by goal-setting and planning. If you want something, you assess where you are now and where you want to be. Then you map out the steps to get from A to B, draw up an action-plan and start confidently striding out in the direction of your dreams. This is a wonderful notion, but it's based on two assumptions that are simply not true for many people.

The first is that you know clearly what "the good life" is. However, many people have very little idea what "really good" feels like. If most of your life has been average, or fairly ho-hum, it can be very hard to even imagine a life that feels different. Psychologists have discovered that one year after winning large amounts of money on lotteries, most people are no happier than they were before. They have a lot more possessions, a bigger house and a more luxurious lifestyle, but inside themselves, they feel much the same as they ever did. Only the outside has changed.

The second assumption is that what you want is "stuff" - something you can see, hear, feel and measure. You want cars or boats or houses or money. You want to be CEO of the company.

You want a shapely body with only 8% body-fat or you want a better job than your obnoxious cousin.

But what if your goal is to become your highest and best self? What if your deepest heart's desire is to fulfil the greatness you sense within yourself - to recognise and overcome your own limiting beliefs and to step up to living your life more authentically? How do you come up with an action plan for that?

It's like asking a rosebud to come up with an action plan for becoming an opened rose. In outline, the answer is "soak up the sun and rain, relax, put no impediment in the way and the open bloom will arise from your own nature." The rosebud doesn't need to know in what order its petals should open nor by how many degrees they should open at which time.

It's the same with us. Becoming who you are, at the deepest level of your being is not something you can write an action plan for. Logical planning will not speed up the process or make it easier. When you begin, not only do you not know what "the finished product" will look like, you almost definitely have a skewed idea of where you are starting from. If you could clearly see who you are right now, the job would be half-done!

So it's OK to not know. It's OK not to have a plan. It's OK to operate by feel - by tuning in to the love and peace and truth inside you and to just keep moving in that direction. In fact, you can't align with your deepest Self any other way. As you become more aware of making choices in each moment, you can increasingly choose to tune in to the oasis of peace and love in your centre and to live life from that space. This isn't about getting somewhere - it's about choosing to focus on being the clearest version of yourself in each moment.

LETTING YOUR LIGHT SHINE OUT

I came across this idea some years ago in some Sufi writing and it has stayed with me because it is such a beautiful metaphor.

These particular Sufis say that when each of us is created, Allah writes our True Name on our heart, in letters of light. Our task in life is to become so clear and transparent that everyone can see what our True Name is - who we were created to be.

But this is not the kind of change you can easily turn into a Vision Board or a set of affirmations. Even if you can imagine to some extent how it might feel to be such a deeper, more centred version of yourself, what does that look like?

How is it different from how your life looks now?

You may have a strong feeling about the direction your life should be moving in:
- I know I want to be a healer.
- I feel a calling to create films that will make people think differently about themselves.
- I want to write a book that will change how people relate to the planet.
- I need to be an advocate for disadvantaged people.
- I want to teach Peaceful Living.
- I'd love to be a truly amazing parent and help my kids grow up happy and fulfilled.
- I'm really drawn to work with sick animals.

Even then, you may have very little idea about what that will look like in your life. And you may have even less idea about how to make it happen.

How do you become a "Peaceful Living Teacher," for example? The job-title doesn't even exist. Your local college probably does not have a vocational programme in Teaching Peaceful Living 101. There are no qualifications.
There is no career route. It's not at all obvious who you should ask about it. Do you know anyone doing similar work? Probably not.

You may not want to change what you do at all. Your work may be deeply fulfilling to you already and it may seem like a good match with the deeper version of yourself that you sense from time to time, and feel called to become. So how does _your_ life look different in the future? How can you create a vision of a future in which things look much the same, but the feeling is different, because you're living from a deeper level?

Again, what if you are a person who has never lived their life in a linear, goal-setting kind of way? For you, it may well be that much of the joy in life lies in the journey of discovery. You may be on a spiritual path that strongly emphasizes "Letting go, and Letting God." How does goal-setting sit with that? Not well at all, if you are like many of the people I have talked to. And yet, it's not that you don't care how your life turns out.

You almost certainly want to be happy and fulfilled, but you're prepared to let go of fixed ideas of what that might look like and instead trust in Divine Guidance to keep you on the right path.

So how do you make choices in each moment that keep you moving forwards in the direction of the most joyful life and the deepest growth when you are not completely clear what you are aiming at? How do you "read the signposts" if you don't know what your destination looks like? More importantly, how can you experience joy and growth right now, in the only time you have?

The key learning is to focus on who you are becoming.

CHAPTER 5: WHO WANTS IT?

What's the difference between Character and Personality?

The word personality comes from the Latin word *persona*. This referred to the wooden masks worn by actors in Roman dramas. So in its most basic meaning it has a sense of being a false face, something we are pretending to be. The personality is something we construct throughout our lifetime. It's like the celebrities who make conscious decisions about which designer labels to wear. They are creating an image and then living up to it.

The word character comes from an ancient Greek word *kharakter*, meaning an engraved mark. This had a subsidiary meaning of being a mark on the soul. So the idea behind character is similar to the Sufi idea of Allah/God engraving our true name on our heart in letters of Light. Character, unlike Personality, is about our Real Selves.

Who's here, now?

If the physicists and the mystics are right, and somehow time doesn't exist - it's just the way our brains process our lives - then all of you exists right here, now. So does that mean that pre-destination is true?

Has God somehow decided every detail of your life in advance, so now you're a puppet, living out a story that has already been completely written? After all, if your whole life is somehow here, now, that surely includes the end of the story? Surely this idea abolishes the whole notion of free will?

It's more complex than that. How the physicists see it, is that every possibility exists now. Somewhere in the multiverse of possibilities there is a version of you who takes every one of those paths fanning out from now. You get to choose which version of you actually makes it into concrete, everyday reality. When you choose, you collapse the other choices and those alternative lives wink out.

The choice in each moment is who will you become? Which world will you open to? That's the lived reality behind what the physicists are saying. Every possibility is packed into each second. Creation seems to be constructed like one of those branching fiction books:
    "The dragon is in the corridor. What do you do?
- Run for the hills. (Go to page 92)
- Pull out your sword. (Go to page 40)

- Drink the Potion of Invisibility."(go to page 66)

Every possibility is enfolded, implicate. I can get to any outcome - so long as I choose an appropriate sequence of paths.

Every version of your life is a possibility. However you live it, it will be your life. The level on which you want to play is entirely your choice. When I was pregnant with my eldest daughter, I taught myself Astrology. I reasoned that if I knew right from her birth what to expect, I'd be better prepared. I have to say that I found it helpful, even though I never became very good at it.

The really fascinating bit for me was getting the whole big picture of Astrology - the idea that right from the first moment of life we are all different. We are not born as "blank pages." I think most parents would agree with this, even without knowing anything at all about Astrology! Right from square one, we have something to contribute to the whole that nobody else, anywhere, has done in quite the same way. There has never been anybody else exactly like us. Our Gift is unique and can be expressed in different ways, at different levels.

Even if someone is born at the exact same second as you, the difference in the place of birth will change their birth-chart. The astrology chart is almost like a musical score - the song of your life. Whatever you do, it will be a version of that tune - but it's totally up to you how you perform it.

Each of us can express our Gift at different levels. If you have a talent for music, you might get to be a famous concert pianist. However, the same pattern could be expressed by you singing karaoke at a party, joining a marching band, jamming with a bunch of mates or even by singing in the shower. It could be also be expressed by you composing wonderful music that made people weep when they heard it. Or by you being one of these singers who turns up on TV programs like The X-Factor, looking totally ordinary and then who then steps up to the mike, opens their mouth and has the whole audience on their feet, cheering, clapping and crying , in about a minute flat. You get to choose the level you want to play at.

So the challenge for each of us is how could I take my life and my talents to the next level? And this is not just about obvious, generally recognised talents like music or art.

Maybe your real gift is invisible - you can't sing or perform in any way but you're an amazing friend or naturally kind or skilled at listening. Perhaps you are a born healer or one of those people who seem to emanate peace wherever they go. You may have green fingers or an ease and skill when dealing with animals. You could have a feeling for wood or stone that leads you to create wonderful structures that enhance the lives of the people who use them.

It doesn't matter. There's a Jewish saying that on the Day of Judgement, God won't ask you why you weren't more like Moses. He'll ask why you weren't more like you.

Which brings us to the question - Who <u>are</u> you?

Seeing my Self
I remember the first time I saw something of my Real Self in meditation. Just like the meditation I talked about in the prologue, my meditation suddenly "went deep" on me. I entered a very still and vast space. It was difficult to tell if it was inside me or if I was inside it.

 I began to feel very centred in myself, as if I was getting a coherent sense of myself in a way I hadn't experienced before.

Suddenly, I saw myself as I appeared to be here, within this out-of-time place - as a being made of light. I didn't have a body with arms and legs; I just seemed to exist as a complex form of patterned light. My essence was joyful, loving and enthusiastically creative. The experience didn't last long, but it was very clear.

Afterwards, two things struck me about it. The first was, that my Real Self had none of the faults for which I continually beat myself up. It wasn't sarcastic, or cynical. It didn't have rage inside it. It wasn't mean. It didn't feel jealous of others. It didn't tell white lies. It was just radiant, joyful, creative and loving.

On the other hand, it didn't seem to have many of the attributes I was so proud of in myself. It wasn't witty or entertaining. It didn't have a high IQ. It wasn't a good mimic or a particularly fast learner. It was just radiantly joyful, creative and loving.

I found the meditation very disorienting. How could all those personality faults be somehow unreal? How could my witty repartee be profoundly unimportant to who I am? (I didn't feel moved to stop doing it because it's great fun and it clearly wasn't a denial or a betrayal of who I am but it was just completely irrelevant.)

Furthermore, if I am radiant, joyful, creative and loving - if I am really an eternal being of light - what happens to all my excuses? Most of them disappear in an instant.

I have to start taking responsibility for the way I am. I have to recognise that <u>whatever</u> has happened to me in my life, it hasn't dimmed the light of who I am. It may have savagely shaken my belief that I could be more than my everyday self. It might have temporarily convinced me that I was a victim of difficult circumstances, from which I couldn't ever expect to be fully healed. It might have given me an all-encompassing life-story, an interesting personality, an endless internal drama that saps my energy. Nevertheless, on a Real level, my Self is untouched - still radiant, still loving.

This must be one of the most difficult things to recognise about yourself. It's one reason that so many people resist any notion that on some level they are still the perfect being they were created to be. It's more difficult to integrate your greatness than it is to see your flaws or to uncover another chapter of your drama.
The religions of the Western world have been telling us for thousands of years that we are worthless sinners.

Psychoanalysis has introduced us all to the idea that our subconscious mind is full of murderous, incestuous and rage-filled impulses. We have no problem, generally, with accepting that deep within there might be a whole lot of darkness that we really don't want to examine too closely.

But accepting inner greatness? That is beyond the "possibility horizon" for most of us. We may have a sneaking suspicion that even to consider such things could be a sign of mental imbalance. If I start to believe there is greatness within me, what's to stop me coming to believe I'm Napoleon?

If it's not a sign of madness, there may be a guilty fear that believing in our inner greatness could be sinful in itself. Surely it shows a sickening lack of humility? In truth, all of these are excuses we make to prevent ourselves looking at the truth about who we are. Because part of us senses that once you have seen it, you can't un-see it. You can't un-know who you are. It changes your sense of who you are forever and it shoots all your excuses to bits.

Sudden Seeing
Radical change is not a part of the story for most people.

Yet there are people everywhere who have experienced their lives being transformed in an instant and their sense of identity changed forever.

People have near-death experiences and <u>see</u> that angels exist and the afterlife is real. They can't un-see that, and the knowing changes them. Other people get hit by lightning, frozen in snow-drifts, almost drowned - and come back different, aware of a deeper reality behind normality. Or they go to see a healer and experience a "miraculous" cure of some illness or injury that had been assumed to be unchangeable. All their friends and family focus on the great physical change - the cancer has gone, they can hear, their vision has been restored, they can walk again - but behind that, the healed person may sense that something deep in their sense of self has shifted. Not just their body, but their identity has been transformed.

Or, like mystics throughout the ages, people have visions. Sometimes this is after a lifetime of intense prayer or meditation, but it does seem occasionally to happen out of the blue, to quite ordinary people.

I remember in my teens meeting an elderly gentleman who had had the same prayer routine for all of his adult life. He would read a short passage from the Bible, then kneel and pray for maybe 10 minutes. Finally he would sit quietly, in an attitude of listening, telling God that he was finished talking for now and if God had anything to say to him, he was ready to hear it.

Normally, he'd just sit for 10 minutes or so, during which time he often noticed the solutions to everyday problems popping up in his mind. He accepted these insights as God's answer to his prayers and generally found them useful and relevant.

Except that one day, something else had happened. For no reason that he could identify, the elderly gentleman had found himself transported in consciousness into a vast space full of the most brilliant light. He could sense angels all around him and could hear the sound of what he took to be angelic singing - a wonderful, unearthly music of incredible beauty and harmony. There was an amazing smell, too, he said, which he could never afterwards quite recapture, but perhaps like incense. And there was something else - a deep presence that he took to be the Holy Spirit, something so wonderful there were no words to describe it.

In telling me this he was close to tears, still deeply moved by the memory of it, even though it had happened months before. The elderly man had no explanation for any of this but assumed he had just been given a preview of Heaven. It was all very wonderful, he said, but it had changed his life in ways that were hard to integrate.

The comfortable religion he had grown old with could not explain it, or even contain it. His pastor was baffled. His friends and family were no help. Neither was I. At that time I knew no-one else who had experienced anything similar and although I had read many books about mystical experiences, to me they were just ideas - lovely ideas perhaps, but completely outside my reality.

That apparently chance encounter served a deep purpose for me, though, because it showed me that mystical visions weren't just for medieval saints. People were experiencing them <u>now</u>. And they still are. Nowadays , you can go to any reasonable-sized high street book store and find books by people who have talked to angels, had near-death experiences, visited Heaven or had some kind of "close encounter" with the Sacred World.

Either mysticism is becoming an epidemic, or people are just more prepared to talk about such things. That Sacred World, that timeless dimension, still underlies the world we live in. And more people than ever before are contacting it, even if only once or twice in their lifetime, and being changed forever by it.

One thing on which mystics are agreed is that the Reality that underlies the everyday world is beautiful. It's full of Light and Love. Once you've seen it, you can never again believe that "Life is out to get you", even when disasters are happening all around you in your life. You've seen the space where this all makes sense. You know there is an deep love and immense compassion behind everything. Even if you've only ever glimpsed it once, that seeing changes things forever. The knowing and the seeing transforms you and your life.

You can never again get quite so lost in the daily drama of your life. Your fear of Death loses its edge. And you know, bone-deep, that there is more to you and to your life than meets the eye. What's more, you know that this is true for everyone. All of us in some sense belong to the world of light. It is our true country. All of us have an inner identity that is so much more than the outer one. We are all capable of extraordinary things.

It's happening <u>now</u>
And this inner identity is in us all right now. It's something we already are. It's not something we have to work out.

If you want to be a celebrity, or a successful business-person, you have to put a great deal of thought into creating that. What kind of clothes should you wear? Which are the designer labels that have the most impact? These shoes or those? This watch or that one? You need to think about which restaurants you want to be seen in, which holiday spots to visit, even which charities you should ideally be seen to be supporting.

To be your Real Self, what you mostly have to do is let go of all the unreal stories you have taken on. The process is more like an archaeological dig than a building site. You don't have to construct your Real Self, just let go of attachment to the false one. You don't even need to take it to pieces or get rid of it. Just see through it. See beyond it.

Discovering your Real Self is not a total mystery. Throughout our lives we get clues as to who we really are. Just think for a minute about the situations and people that bring out the best in you. The next chapter looks at this in more depth.

CHAPTER 6: ARE YOU SHINING?

Discovering your Real Self

Discovering your Real Self, to any extent at all, is the most deeply fulfilling thing you can do. You're intrinsically set up to find the Real to be beautiful and fascinating. There's something deeply satisfying about getting in touch with your Self. It fulfils a longing in you that you may not even have recognised up until now.

The feeling is something like when you have a word "at the tip of your tongue" but you can't remember it. Suddenly, probably when you're doing something completely different and not thinking about the annoying word at all, it pops into your head. How do you know it's the right word, the one you were looking for? You just know. It ticks some kind of internal box. There's a feeling of rightness about it. You don't need someone else to tell you you've got the right word.

In the same way, when you touch the Real in yourself - or even begin to get close to it - you don't need someone else to tell you that you're right. The experience feels right. There's a kind of internal **aha!** Some circuit in yourself is completed.

Just as completing an electric circuit is what turns on an electric light, whenever you are moving towards your Real Self, you light up. So one way to discover your Real Self and your Gift is to start to look at the things in life that make you light up.

What makes you light up?

There's a famous quote from Howard Thurman:

> "Don't ask what the world needs. Ask what makes you come alive and go do it. Because what the world needs is people who have come alive."

You've almost definitely met people who seem to be lit up, shining and truly alive in this way. I remember a bus driver who drove one of the small local buses that rambled around a housing estate, picking up mostly young parents and elderly people who wanted to get to the shops. It was a tedious, slow journey endlessly meandering along minor roads and with frequent stops. The same people tended to catch the bus most days. It was clear that the bus driver had a friendly relationship with many of them. He laughed and joked and enquired after sick children. Most surprisingly, he sang at the top of his voice for much of the time.

Occasionally, passengers would shout comments on the singing or suggest he do it more quietly. "Just bringing a little sunshine into your day," he would reply. It was very clear that, on the whole, he was successful. He was a small bright spot in the day for many of his passengers.

The journey stayed in my mind because, generally, bus drivers are not people I associate with being shining. It's not often that they seem to be lit up and alive with the joy of driving buses - in fact, this is the only shining bus driver I ever remember seeing! But it showed me that probably no job exists that is not an opportunity for some people to shine in doing it.

Do you remember your favourite teacher at school? I would guess that he or she was one of the "truly alive" teachers - the ones who teach from a passion for their subject and a deep care for their pupils. Have you met a doctor or a nurse who seemed to emanate healing energy? - the kind of person who made you feel safe and cared for from the moment they walked into the room? Do you know a craftsman or woman who lights up telling you about the beautiful grain in this wood? Or as they invite you to appreciate the way this fabric catches the light? Or who points out to you the depths in this coloured glaze?

It's not only professionals or artists who shine at their work, though. As well as the singing bus driver, I remember a street cleaner who worked in the small town where I lived some years ago. He was clearly learning-disabled but was fortunate to have found a job at which he could excel. He cleaned those streets like no other street cleaner I have ever seen, paying attention to every tiny piece of rubbish and clearing away every single bit. As he worked, he smiled frequently, clearly taking pleasure in doing a good job.

Then there are the people who simply shine in the way they live. Whether they are employed or not, they seem to pour out their Gift. You'll have met people like this. Their Gifts may be different, but the feeling of rightness and inner contentment about them is similar. You get the sense that here is someone with a solid centre, someone who is truly alive, appreciating life on a deeper level from most people.

Have you met these Gifts?
Do you recognise any of these?
- The person who is "A Presence of Peace" - who simply seems to fill every room with calm and peacefulness. Quarrels die down or get resolved when they are around, hot tempers get soothed, upsets get sorted out.

They may be a nursery teacher, a lawyer, a healing professional - or simply a waitress, a barman, a grandparent, or a good friend.

- The person who is "A Deep Listener." When they listen to you, you feel heard on every level. It feels as if they are taking in more than just your words. Somehow, as they listen, they hold all of you and all of your life in their hands. You find yourself letting go of grief and anger you have held for years, and finding answers to long-lasting problems emerging apparently by themselves. This person could be a counsellor, a psychologist, a vicar - or it may just be a stranger in a cafe.

- The person who is "A Beacon of Joy." These people seem to glow from the inside. Their joy doesn't seem to have a cause in the circumstances of their life - they are not usually wealthy, or famous, or even necessarily successful in their career. They seem to be able to find a blessing , or at least hope, in difficult times and find something to be genuinely grateful for even in the face of problems. They are rare treasures, wherever you find them.

- The person who is "A Never-ending Spring of Practical Creativity." These are the people you go to for real-life solutions.

Want a wedding breakfast for 300 people, half of whom are dairy-intolerant , some of whom are vegetarian, and the rest of whom are cattle-farmers? They can do it. Or want a baby's pushchair/stroller that steers well, even when loaded with shopping and you only have one hand free to manoeuvre it? Do you need an idea for your business launch? Or a fuel that causes no pollution? They're working on it.

- The "Fountain of Inspiration." Whenever you lose sight of the Big Picture this person reminds you of the greater truths you have forgotten. They fire you up with enthusiasm, give you a new vision of what could be possible, and remind you of what's really important to you. They may be a religious preacher or minister, but could just as easily be a coach, a motivational speaker, or your Auntie Bess.

- The "Pillar of Integrity." These are people who just do what is right, even when that is the difficult choice. They may do this so quietly that it may take you a while to notice, until slowly it occurs to you that here is someone who truly walks their talk. Occasionally, these people emerge into the public eye, championing the cause of right action - and then you get a Gandhi, a Martin Luther King or one of the whistle-blowers who lose their jobs in

Government or Public Service when they tell the truth about some injustice or corruption behind the scenes. Often, it seems the real Gift of these people is the effect they have on the people who know them, work with them or even simply meet them. These people are so transparently honest, so unswervingly true to their values, that - even when we disagree with them - they call us all to a higher standard of integrity.

There are many more. You may have recognised yourself in some of the descriptions or suddenly found a fitting label for someone else that you know.

Once you start looking for Gifts, it gets easier to spot them. You get into the habit of labelling what it is that is special about someone. You also become increasingly able to identify your own Gifts - and to own them, treasure them and nurture them. You start making a commitment to let your light shine out instead of hiding it where nobody ever sees it - including yourself! Learning to do this will give you the richest possible life, beyond any conventional definitions of success. Make a promise to yourself today to explore what makes you shine.

Money and Your Gift

Your Gift is not necessarily anything to do with money. There's a saying that's popular in a lot of Success literature:

"Do what you love and the money will follow."

Maybe. But what if what you love the most is going for long walks in the countryside, totally alive with the joy of walking and a deep appreciation of the beauty of the natural world? Or hanging out in coffee shops, having inspiring conversations with total strangers? (Whose lives you may have changed - but you may never know how; certainly, the interactions don't presently carry any kind of paid-for work label such as "Counselling" or "Life Coaching.")

It's definitely possible to find ways that you can incorporate these into a source of income. However, it won't necessarily just "follow" without some clear and structured action on your part. So it's possible to have an income that is not connected to your Gift and it's possible to have a Gift that is not connected to an income.

The ideal happens when, either by ingenuity or through chance, you find a way to make a good livelihood from living your Gift.

But it's not essential that you do. We all need to eat and to keep a roof over our heads.
I am most certainly not suggesting that you need to throw away all your security in order to live your Gift. Nonetheless, it's important not to fill up your life so full with making a living that you have no time to create a life that is worth living for. The more you can live in a way that expresses your Gift, the richer and more meaningful your life experience becomes.

There is sometimes an emphasis in New Age circles on how it is OK to make money - and even a lot of money - from your spiritual work. I think this may be a necessary counter-balance to the insistence for the last 2,000 years that spirituality means poverty. However, it's important not to equate money alone with abundance. There is much more to having a rich life than simply having money.

Joy, gratitude, an awareness of the presence of God, a loving family, opportunities to learn and grow, the time to rest and appreciate the beauty of the natural world, all these are important. Money is a valued part of this and can be seen as a gift from God. But <u>all</u> of life is a gift, a love-affair with the Divine - if we choose to live it that way.

Money is good to have, but although it can fill up your pockets and your bank account in a nice way, it doesn't fill your heart, because your heart was made for a richer diet. Your heart longs for the Authentic Life.
I think this quote says it all:

> "Some people are so poor, that all they have is money."

On the other hand, some people are so rich on the inside that, even though they may have very little material wealth, they light up their world.

Can you "Fake It until you Make It?"
A common piece of advice in Success literature is to "fake it until you make it." The idea is that if you act as if you are happy, you'll become happy; if you act as if you are successful, you'll become successful.

This is largely true - you've already seen that your subconscious mind has difficulty telling the difference between real-life experiences and those which are intensely imagined. You can "fake yourself" happier. You can "act as if" you're confident - and find that, amazingly, you _are_ more confident.

However, you can't fake being authentic. You can't pretend to be Real. By its very nature, authenticity has to be authentic. Reality has to be Real. You've probably met people who are trying to fake authenticity. I certainly have and they tend to send shivers down my spine.

You may have met them as:

- Religious cultists or members of fundamentalist groups who are explaining how they - and only they - hold the keys to salvation which have set them free to be smilingly happy in a way that doesn't quite reach their eyes.

- Multi-level Marketing representatives who are telling you about the unbelievably, radiantly, wonderful life they now enjoy through using and selling seaweed juice or magnetic earrings or supplements made from rare volcanic dust - all of this while maintaining eye contact with an intensity associated with alien life-forms in movies who are trying to take over your brain.

- Devotees of high-powered coaches or motivational speakers who tell you how they have achieved multi-million pound incomes by following only 4 simple steps - all delivered with the kind of throbbing vocal intensity that gives the word "Success" about an extra 2 or 3 syllables.

Authenticity has to come from your heart. It can't come from an idea of how Authentic People would act.

When you fake authenticity, it shows. Your smile may spread from ear to ear, but it doesn't quite reach your eyes. Your voice may throb with emotion, but somehow it sounds "spot off." There's something about it that doesn't ring true. Your handshake may be firm and warm, but there's something about the energy it conveys that sends prickles down the back of people's necks. You're fake, and people can tell.

When you are focused in your Self, speaking the truth directly from your heart, acting towards people with a real kindness and care that is not pretended, doing something you love with a real passion, you don't have to practice your handshake or how to look people frankly in the eye when you speak.

You are Real. You resonate with the energy of Truth. People know. And your in-tune energy tends to bring out the best in them. As you shine, you light up other people.

Your integrity draws out the truth in them. Your joy raises their spirits. You can make a genuine difference just by walking down the street. You can change the world, one tiny interaction at a time. Faking it can never achieve that.

Making a difference by how you cook the rice

Some years ago, I visited a Hare Krishna ashram in Birmingham (UK). I was with a group of people who were engaging in spiritual exploration, visiting various spiritual groups, trying new meditation and prayer practices and generally learning to appreciate the multi-cultural traditions of the city.

Some of the evening was very much as I had expected. There was a lot of devotional chanting. There was a reading from the Bhagavad Gita. There was an introductory talk, explaining some of the basic beliefs for the benefit of the visitors. And, last of all, there was a meal.

The devotees of Lord Krishna believe that food that has been cooked in a spirit of love for the Lord, and that has been offered to Him, has sacred qualities and blesses the people who eat it. So it's part of their tradition to offer ashram visitors a meal, made in this way.

The food is simple - a couple of different vegetarian curries, lentil dhal and brown rice. I hadn't expected this and was slightly embarrassed by it. The meals came out already plated up, so there was no opportunity to turn down the brown rice.

Having been "On the Spiritual Path" in the 1970s, I'd eaten a lot of brown rice. Way too much to my mind; brown rice is tricky to cook well and easily goes soggy and sticky. Even when it's well-cooked, my body seems to find it heavy and rather indigestible. So I left it until last and ate the curries and dhal. They were pleasant enough in a somewhat bland way.

Krishna devotees believe that onions and garlic can inflame lust and so miss them out of monastic cooking, replacing them with a spice called *hing*. (I've no idea what that is in English.) As someone who flavours most of my meals with well-browned onions, I found the lack of them a little odd, but interesting.
It became apparent that leaving food on the plate was likely to be seen as impolite, so I started on the brown rice - and had one of the most amazing experiences of my life.

I don't know who had cooked that rice - but they were definitely the most spiritually advanced soul in the ashram.

That rice had been cooked with so much love and devotion that I could feel golden light pouring out from it and spreading through my mouth. I assure you, this is not a normal experience for me. I had never experienced it before, and haven't since.

But every single mouthful of brown rice was spreading waves of golden light into my mouth and throughout my body. It was an intense sensation. The rice had been cooked with so much love that the love poured out of it. I sat and ate it, utterly awed.

That experience really taught me something about making everyday work a sacred service. What if hospital food was cooked like this? Don't you think it would have an effect on the patients? What if food was cooked like this in prisons? In schools? In workplace cafeterias? In homes? We could change the lives of the people we lived with and worked with by how we cooked their dinner!

What if we built homes like this, imbuing every brick with positive energy? What would happen if we put energy like this into the design of household appliances, cars, public spaces, children's toys? What would it be like to live in a world where every person worked like this?

How could our children and young people be changed if they were taught like this, brought up like this, surrounded by this shining, loving energy from conception onwards?

What might be the effect on the great ecological problems of today - global warming, deforestation, pollution, and the extinction of so many other species if all of us started treating ourselves and all the life around us with this type of care and attention? Living and working from the heart, we can change the world by putting a different energy into every day.
What kind of world will you choose to live in?

CHAPTER 7: CHANGING THE WORLD

Bringing In The Aquarian Paradigm

It seems clear that we are in a transition between two great eras of time. If you're into Astrology, we're moving from the Piscean age to the Aquarian age. However, even if you're not a believer in Astrology, you've only got to look around you to realise how much, and how fast things have been changing since the middle of the 19th century.

Before the 19th Century, most people led lives that were almost the same as their parents and grandparents. Change was so slow, you might barely register it over a lifetime. Then - within a space of 200 years or so - came the agricultural revolution, industrialisation, mass transportation, mass education, modern medicine, technology, and the ongoing communication revolution. Alongside that there have been big shifts in consciousness. I'll refer to the transition in astrological terms because it provides a convenient label for the shift, but you don't have to accept Astrology to follow what I'm saying.

For 2000 years or so, during the Piscean age, the material world has been largely seen as the enemy of the spiritual life. What has been the most accepted route to get spiritual realisation? To go into a cave or a desert or a deep forest. To lock yourself up in a monastery or a convent. To get away from people.

The aim has been to turn off the input from your body so that you can let go of your awareness of it. So you'd starve yourself - and maybe even hurt yourself. Flog yourself from time to time. Lie on a bed of nails. Hold one arm up in the air until it withers and you can't use it any more. Sleep on rocks. The whole emphasis has been to get away from this material world, away from the body, and lift your consciousness up and out.

The material world came to be seen as sticky and deluding - give it half a chance and you'd be over your head in temptation you couldn't resist. It would suck you in. Enjoy a meal, savouring the taste of the food and you'd be entrapped by the sin of Gluttony. Take an extra five minutes in bed and Slothfulness would enslave you. God/Truth was generally seen as out there, up there - anywhere but here, in the midst of ordinary life.

The true reward of a spiritual life was to get away from this one. You'd get a better grade of marble throne in Heaven. Or you'd step off the wheel of karma and never have to incarnate here ever again. You'd merge with Light and melt into a cosmic ocean of bliss. You'd get to dwell in an afterlife of joy and beauty.

The material world was not your problem. It was full of suffering to persuade people to discover spiritual truths. Or it was a Vale of Tears, designed to test the faith of the Chosen Few. If you did something about the suffering you'd slow down other people's spiritual growth. You wanted other people to get to Heaven or to achieve Enlightenment, didn't you? So let them suffer.

Suffering purified the soul. Cheerful acceptance of difficulties strengthened faith. There was no point trying to make society fairer. People were born into their situation because of past karma or the will of God. It would all come out in the wash. They might get a better deal next lifetime. or they'd get a payoff for their suffering in Heaven. Or, if they didn't accept the suffering with sufficient humility, they could just burn in Hell for all eternity - but, hey, you'd told them. Their stupidity and spiritual reluctance weren't your problem.

I realise there have been exceptions from this - monasteries that ran hospitals, philanthropists who opened schools and libraries and sought to better the lives of the poor, saints that healed the sick and religious leaders who stressed the value of everyday life - but I'm looking at the Big Picture here and on the whole, the emphasis for a long time has been on transcending the material world.

But right now, I perceive that there is a major shift in spiritual awareness happening. Increasingly, instead of lifting their consciousness up and out and just seeking to merge with a transcendent reality, spiritual people are raising their consciousness to higher levels. They are then bringing those high level energies and insights back into everyday life and working to change the world.

Instead of escaping from Earth into Heaven/Enlightenment, they are seeking to experience Divine energies and to ground them here on Earth. This is the era of embodied spirituality. Increasingly, people who see themselves as being on a spiritual path are being drawn to make a difference in the world.

Often the way they feel drawn to make this difference is not just to add their energies to existing systems, but by changing the paradigms on which the systems are based. This isn't just a devoted effort to do more of the same. This is a revolutionary awareness of a different way of doing things altogether.

The astrological sign for the Age of Pisces was two fish, swimming in opposite directions. So maybe it's not surprising that spirituality in this age has not been very practical - after all, fish are not noted for their ability to have both feet on the ground!

This has been an era where saints levitated in ecstasy, shone with unearthly Light, went off into altered states of consciousness for days and weeks at a time, and generally lost track of everyday activities like regular mealtimes. It's been a good time for floating in bliss, but not perhaps such a good time for noticing what we are collectively doing to the planet and taking active steps to care for the natural world on which all our lives depend. On the whole, it's not been a good time either for tuning into our bodies and learning how to activate our own innate instincts for wellbeing and healing.

Instead, particularly in the Western world, we've developed highly sophisticated medicine based on turning off all our body's signals to us that something is out of balance. Got a pain? Take an aspirin. Head filling up with mucus, and making you sneeze and cough? Take a decongestant. Some part of your body playing up? Surgically remove it.

This kind of medicine could only be developed in a society that sees bodies primarily as the vehicles for carrying our minds around in. The attitude seems to have been that bodies are OK, in a grudging kind of way - but you wouldn't want to actually _live_ in them.

I see the coming Age of Aquarius as being very different. The astrological sign for Aquarius is a man carrying a pot of water which he is pouring out. This is spirituality made practical. This is a person who sees thirsty people or who sees wilting crops, fills a jug of water and pours it out where it's needed. It's not a person whose response to pain and suffering is to pray about it and ask God to sort it all out. This is a person who believes that God has already populated the planet with more than 7 billion solutions to the world's problems. This is someone who believes that part of their spiritual path is to find the problem that they are uniquely equipped to solve and go fix it.

The Story of Buckminster Fuller

Buckminster Fuller was one of the most prolific and successful inventors of the 20th century. Among other things, he invented a composting toilet, the geodesic dome, and the World Game - designed to teach the attitudes and strategies that would promote world peace.

His strategy for success? He said that before inventing anything, he would mentally ask God what in the world most needed inventing next - and would then wait for inspiration. I believe that this is the kind of approach that exemplifies the Aquarian age - working from an inner connection to inspiration and the kind of wide-open creativity that can think right outside all of the established ways of doing things to come up with something totally new.

I see many more of us bringing in truly innovative solutions to the current problems in health, energy, conservation, education, justice, transportation, and work - resulting in the creation of a balanced and harmonious world that works for everyone. Part of this will be a new way of working, tapping in to our own well-springs of inspiration and creativity but also to insight and guidance from higher levels.

It's about a way of working that moves from the inside out, rather than trying to solve problems from the middle of the mind-set that created them in the first place. So, let's get started!

CHAPTER 8: BEGIN NOW!

Changing yourself begins Now

Change begins now - because it can't begin at any other time. Right now, there is no future to make glorious or a past you need to overcome. If you can't live authentically right now, when will you do it? You only have now. Now is a powerful time to change your life - in fact, it's the only time you have real power to do anything.

Right this moment, in this <u>now</u>, you are being created anew. Every instant is a time of new beginning and renewal at the deepest possible level. Whatever and whoever you have been up until now, you can change. One of the great discoveries of 20th Century physics was that time doesn't exist. We usually experience time unfolding in a linear way because of the way our brains make sense of the world, but mystics through the ages have had breakthrough moments where they have seen that behind the unfolding story of everyday life, there is a vast timeless dimension from which everything unfolds anew in each second.

Theologians have argued with scientists in the past about how long ago it was that Creation took place, but the Truth is that Creation is happening <u>now</u>. It has never stopped happening.

Normally, the inertia built in to our information-processing systems causes us to carry forward a consistent way of looking at things so that life seems to us to be a seamless narrative. We are born, we grow from being babies to being children, then through adolescence to adulthood, and finally to old age and death. Throughout this we are ourselves, the same as yesterday, except another day older and more experienced.

But if, as the physicists are saying, time doesn't exist, and every possible version of you is present in this moment, there is enormous potential to change track - to become a greater version of yourself. It may be that this ability is only limited by how much you can let go of the stories you have been holding onto about who you are. As I mentioned earlier, some people seem able to undergo instantaneous enormous changes that we often term as "miracles." What happens?

How does someone undergo a so-called miraculous level of change? It seems that on some level, they are able to let go of their existing story - just drop it completely. In a second, they stop tightly holding the story that says "I am a victim of tragic circumstances. I had this terrible illness/ accident/birth defect happen to me and now I am diminished - a lesser self, a damaged self."

Some kind of inner shift of perception happens and they see a deeper truth. "I am whole and complete. I have never been otherwise. Every cell in my body is created from Light and reflects the radiance of the Divine." They swap tracks in that instant.

But to do that, they have to be fully present, here and now, even if only for a brief time. It may be the first time it has ever happened to them. It may be the <u>only</u> time it ever happens to them! But the power of now is that this is the only time that is 100% real. We tend to think of Eternity as a very long time. But Eternity is what is there when we step outside of time into total immersion in now. All of God/Basic Goodness/The Universe/Divinity is present right now - because this is where Eternity is.

God isn't spread thinly like butter, smeared over interminable lengths of eternity but is intensely and potently present <u>now</u>. So the more you are able to be present right now, the more you enter into the magic of the Real, where Deep Change is truly available.

The Joy of The Game

Being here, fully present, right now is a very simple concept. However, as generations of spiritual practitioners would attest, simple isn't the same thing as easy! Some people do seem to have an instantaneous opening of perception - through drugs or illness or as an out-of-the-blue type of experience that is usually labelled "Grace." But for most people, that opening happens more gradually, through spiritual practice.

The "instantaneous people" show the rest of us that being here now is possible. Spiritual writings from people who have experienced it occasionally, or for most of the time, provide motivation and information. But each of us has to put in the work for ourselves. You can't achieve authenticity by reading about it, any more than you can satisfy your appetite by reading a menu.

Fortunately, being Real is not a "One-stop shop." It's not as if you get to the end of the road and check into the Reality Hotel. There's no stopping place. There's no end point when you've finally arrived. This is an endless journey. So even taking one step along the road feels good. The whole point is not arriving, but travelling.

It's like going to see a sports game - perhaps the final match of the season. You don't buy a ticket for the match and travel to the game just to get the score. You want to know the final score, of course. However, you wouldn't be happy to get there and have the referee decide the outcome of the match by tossing a coin, without so much as a ball being kicked. "Heads it is! So Manchester United have won the FA Cup! Well done, Everton - you came a valiant second!"

You want to see the game. You want to be swept along by the great tide of emotion as your team scores a brilliant goal - or saves one. You want to be a part of that crowd, singing your team's anthem, waving your scarf in your team's colours, encouraging your team's players with chanting and air-horns. You want the emotional highs and lows, the heroic struggle, and hopefully, a dramatic victory.

It's the same with life. We don't come here to relax on the beach, to use an analogy. We come here to have an adventure - to have the time of our lives. We come here to succeed against the odds, to have great fun, to snatch heroic victories from the jaws of defeat. For most people, the journey of life is not like a stroll in the park on a sunny day. It's more like climbing the North face of Everest while wearing roller skates. This is not because our lives are designed by a malign deity. It's because we ourselves enjoy the challenge.

Discovering the Space Between Lifetimes

I assure you, I would never have believed this if I hadn't discovered it for myself. About 20-odd years ago, my life was going through a difficult patch. I felt I was in the wrong job, I wasn't in a relationship and money was tight. I was a single parent of three teenagers and was finding that quite challenging. Generally, life felt pretty grim.

At that time I was still experiencing much of life in Victim Mode. My "sad story" was that bad stuff often happened to me for no good reason that I could see. I was doing the whole classic tirade at God on a regular basis: "Why this? Why me? Why now? Why, why, why?"

Then one day, I had another of those out-of-the-blue meditations. This time, I found myself in a time outside of time, before I was born into this life. I had just finished planning this life. Yes - it was me. I was planning it. Not some malevolent deity. Not some celestial committee. Not some Karmic Parole Board. Me. And I was absolutely delighted with my plan.

If I'd had a physical body at that point, I'd have been grinning all over my face and jumping up and down with excitement. It really felt that good. I felt something like I imagine a top-class athlete feels when they're told they have been picked for their national Olympic team. Or like a first-rate mountaineer who has just been told that the sponsorship deal has come through for their ascent of Everest by the most difficult route.

I was excited in that butterflies-in-the-stomach way when you're anticipating something really thrilling and fantastic. I was overjoyed at the thought of how it would feel to succeed at such a tough challenge.

I had no doubt that this was a real memory on some level - that it had actually happened like that. How do you know if you are remembering something real or imagining something that never happened? You just do.

Once I came out of the meditation, I was completely dumbfounded by what I'd just re-experienced. I found it absolutely astonishing. The only conclusion I could come to was that my Higher Self was totally insane. Why on Earth would I choose such a life for myself? Why would I <u>voluntarily</u> put myself through difficult times? If I'd planned my own life, why hadn't I chosen to win the Lottery and spend the rest of my life in a hammock on some tropical beach?

It took a long time to make sense of what I'd seen and to integrate it. I spent years practising meditation and coming to know myself on a deeper level. And along the way, I began to see that my Real Self was much bigger than my everyday personality self. I was capable of much more than I had believed. I could take on bigger challenges. I was much more courageous. And, even though I'd picked a life full of challenges, I wasn't planning on this being a story of tragic failure - of being defeated by overwhelming forces. My Higher Self was genuinely expecting to succeed.

Now I don't believe I am way ahead of everybody else on the planet. I know I'm unique, but I truly don't think that my uniqueness lies in having bigger goals than everybody else.

I have come to see that all of us are heroes, on the inside. We all have a Higher Self that is a deathless spiritual being, utterly committed to our growth and learning. There really is no such thing as an "ordinary" human being.

For every single one of us, this life is a challenge and an adventure on the spiritual level. Especially given the problems of this time in history, I don't believe that any one of us is here on the planet today by mistake. None of us just stumbled into this. None of us meant to take a package holiday but caught the wrong flight into life and ended up here instead.

No. Every single one of us has the potential to learn and grow into someone wonderful - the clearest, wisest version of who we truly are. As the medieval mystic, Meister Eckhart put it:

> "The seed of God is in us.
> Now, the seed of a pear tree grows into a pear tree -
>
> and a hazel seed grows into a hazel tree;
>
> A seed of God grows into God."

(Translation by Matthew Fox)

Getting in touch with our Real Self
So how do we get in touch with that "seed of God" in us? The answer is through bringing our attention back to here and now - being fully present in each moment. Right here and now is where we can discover and uncover the Real Self within us. Every moment that we can rest in that still, calm centre that lies within, we retune our jangled energies and start coming back into alignment with Reality. As we do so, our life begins to unfold in a magical way.

As I have already said, the outside world is not separate from us on a deep level. So it will always tend to reflect back to us what we are thinking, feeling and believing. We see what we expect to see. We notice people, situations and opportunities that are on a similar frequency to our own. So what kind of world do you think opens out for you as you discover your Real Self and get in tune with it?

The more you come into alignment with the deeper levels of yourself, the more the world "out there" becomes a reflection of the life you came here to lead. You start to notice the openings that allow you to express more of your Gift.

You get a stronger call within you to step up your game and you begin to see how you can be even more authentic and give of yourself from the heart at a deeper level. In other words, you begin to experience a level of fulfilment that is quite new.

It's when you are in touch with your Real Self that you experience being "in the flow." Resting deeply here, you can cook rice and fill it with golden light. Or act as a channel for healing energy to flow through. Or compose music that brings people in contact with their heart. Or create a garden that hums with the feeling of peace, relaxing and healing everybody who walks in it. Or tune into the inspiration that generates the perfect non-polluting fuel, an efficient system of transportation or a housing development that promotes real community.

Many artists, musicians, inventors and sportspeople have talked of entering a "Zone" where it feels as if someone or something else is acting <u>through</u> them. The music seems to be pouring through from somewhere else. It feels as if something or someone else has taken over their body and they can't put a foot wrong as they run like a deer or dance like an angel. Ideas are flowing into their head almost faster than they can write them down.

Poetry is pouring out of their pen. This is what can happen as you get in touch with the Real Self within. But you don't have to wait for random inspiration to strike you. One way to tune into your Real Self is through meditation.

CHAPTER 9: MEDITATION

Learning to Meditate

You may already be practising meditation on a regular basis. But if you aren't, or if you're a complete beginner, don't be put off by an idea that meditation is weird, difficult, or unnatural.

Meditation is as ordinary as eating. Pretty much anybody can do it. (If you're alive, and you're reading this, you qualify!) You don't have to be mystical, spiritual, psychic or even clever to do it. It can be done anywhere – on the bus, in bed, on the toilet or while you're washing up.

It doesn't matter if your "spare time" barely exists, and can be counted in minutes rather than hours. You don't have to change your religion – or even have a religion to change. You don't need any equipment. It doesn't matter if the last time you ever sat cross-legged was in infant school. Children can meditate and so can pensioners, as well as everyone in between.

Although it's certainly possible to meditate for hours, and to enter very deep states of consciousness through meditation, everyday meditation begins by just pulling your attention out of your thoughts and noticing what is happening right here and now, instead.

JUST FOR NOW……

Whatever you're doing right now, take a minute or two to just STOP.
Smile!
Take a deep breath…….and sigh it out.
Let go of all that you've been holding onto today.
Look round you for one beautiful thing. (or person!)
Give thanks in your heart for the beauty in your life, right now.
And then carry on (but just a bit more alive and refreshed!)

What is Meditation?

When you think about meditation, what comes to mind? (Try it now!) Some examples from my meditation class members include:

- Someone sitting cross-legged.
- Burning joss-sticks
- A person chanting – perhaps using an unusual word, such as OM.
- Someone in a leotard.
- A man in yellow robes like a Buddhist monk.

Did any of these images match yours? The truth is that meditation is an experience – it's something you feel inside.

Everything you see and hear when you observe someone meditating is the technique they're using to take them to the experience. It's not the experience itself, which you can't see. Knowing this stops you getting hung-up on techniques. Once you know that all the different ways to meditate are just different paths up the same mountain, you won't worry about whether you should use method A or method B. Use whichever suits you best.

One question I never asked before I started meditation (and which it would have been smart to have asked!) was, what <u>is</u> meditation? The best answer I've found to this so far is "Meditation is paying sustained attention to what is real."
 Which begs the next question - So what is real?

When you're a beginner, what's real involves paying attention to what you're actually doing and sensing, as against what you're imagining or thinking about. Slowly, this focus gets more refined - you notice your body - its tightness, its stuck places, its discomforts. You notice your emotions - anger, jealousy, boredom, irritation. You start to notice your thoughts - <u>as thoughts</u> - and realise that they're just something passing, not part of who you are at all. You begin to notice subtle energies that circulate in and around you.

Someday, sooner or later, behind all of this you notice a silence, even in the middle of sound - or a sense of light, even when it's night time or your eyes are closed - or maybe a still and calm space begins to open up inside you.

You begin to experience Reality (capital R) - and when <u>that</u> begins to happen, something in you realises that this is what you've looked for in everything you've ever done and everything you've ever wanted. With your first taste of Reality - you're hooked! And from then on, however long it takes, you know that you will achieve Oneness with it, because there isn't any other destination for you.

So what's the experience like?

Almost everyone has felt something like meditation, without knowing it. It's something so natural and normal, it seems to be "hard-wired" into how our brains work. You've probably felt it yourself. Do you have a hobby that you get so involved in that you lose track of time? (If not now, this is likely to be something you felt as a child.)

For example, my friend Lynn has an allotment. She'll go there early in the morning, "just for an hour or two." All she intends to do today is to pick the redcurrants.

But while she's collecting the currants, she notices that the spinach needs weeding. Then that the runner beans are ready for picking. After that she decides that, as she's on a roll, she'll plant out the cabbage seedlings. And so it goes, until, suddenly, it's nearly 4pm and she realises that the reason she feels a bit weird is that she hasn't had anything to eat since the ginger biscuits she had with a cup of coffee at 11am!

She's just experienced being in a "flow" state. Some athletes call this state being "in the zone." So what kinds of activities put people in flow? Just look at what people do for their hobbies! Anything from ballroom dancing to stamp collecting can work.

To get into the zone, people run, drive steam engines, paint, rebuild old cars, bake bread, and fly helicopters. To an outsider – a non-enthusiast – some of these activities can seem odd to the point of eccentricity. (Train-spotting and Morris dancing come to mind!) But to an insider, these things are fascinating. Whilst engaged in their hobbies, people feel awake, vibrantly alive, and fully present.

Meditation is like feeling "flow" without having to do the hobby to take you there - which is handy, because you can't take your allotment with you on the Tube! Like the hobby, the meditation technique is a training tool to get you into the zone.

Why all the different methods?
Some people like visual meditations best. They like to focus on a picture or a candle flame. Or they visualise an imaginary scene inside their heads and concentrate on it.

Other people hate meditations like that! They prefer to chant or speak aloud, or maybe to read inspiring words and repeat them internally, letting the meaning sink in.

Still other people can't bear to sit still. They need a meditation where they are moving and focusing on their actions. Then there are those who really enjoy sitting very still in silence, and with their eyes shut, just noticing their breathing. The point is, we're all different.

Your favourite meditation may turn out to be one I don't like very much and vice versa. There's no one "right" way to meditate, that works well for everyone.

You may also find, once you are practising regularly, that you don't want to do the same kind of meditation every time. Something that is calming when you're wound up may send you straight to sleep if you try it when you're very tired. You may usually prefer a quiet, more internal focus, but today, when your mind is very active, you want something with a more external focus to keep you on track. Feel free to experiment! You want to end up with something that works well for <u>you</u> and only you can discover what that is.

I'll keep including occasional meditation techniques **in bold** so that by the end of the book, you should have something that works for you, if you haven't got something already.

LOOKING MEDITATION

A lot of people find it difficult to do the kinds of meditation that involve visualising or vividly imagining things. If this is true for you, you may get on better with a meditation like this one.

1. Find a beautiful object to look at. It needs to be fairly visually complex, like a river-smoothed pebble or a natural crystal - but not a photo, because that will often set you off on chains of associated thoughts.

2. Sit and LOOK at it - really look - for up to 10 minutes. (2 or 3 minutes is fine - this is a beginners' exercise) When you find your mind wandering, bring your attention back to your object. Just look.

3. That's it! When you've had enough, stop!

One piece of advice I would give you if you are just beginning to meditate is not to set yourself up for failure by making meditation unnecessarily difficult for yourself. When I used to teach meditation classes, some of my students said they came home from work all stressed out. They really wanted to use meditation to calm themselves down, but when they tried it, it "didn't work." They couldn't relax and found that they just carried on thinking at 100mph. My suggestion to them was to transition into meditation in a more gradual way.

If you were driving at 100mph, could you stop in two feet? No - you'd need to slow down. Your mind is similar to your car! So do some slowing down activities to decelerate before you meditate. Come into your home and get under a shower - and wash the stresses of the day down the plug-hole. Take your time about it!

Sing, if you like. Or groan out loud - groaning and sighing are wonderful ways to just let go. Go for a run if you prefer. When I feel angry, I love to sweep my stairs - a job I don't do as often as I should! I bang the vacuum cleaner down the stairs, clean the heck out of my carpet, burn off all the adrenaline - and feel utterly virtuous when I reach the bottom! Once I've done that, I'm in a good mood to sit and be still.

Especially when you are a beginning meditator, you don't want to make meditation a hard and horrible duty for yourself. If you do, you'll tend to give up and conclude that meditation really isn't for you. Set yourself up for success!

And finally, for those of you who are more experienced meditators, I'd like to share one of my favourite meditations.

HEART BREATHING MEDITATION
1. Get comfortable - you can sit down, lie down, kneel down or walk.

2. Focus on your heart and feel it start to soften and open.

3. As you breathe in, feel each breath as if you were breathing loving energy and support into your heart.

4. As you breath out, feel each breath as if you were breathing your love and blessings to the world around.

5. Continue - feeling softer, more open, more connected ...until you've had enough.

This was my main meditation for several years and I found that over time my experience got deeper and deeper. I really love this practice - how do you find it?

CHAPTER 10: BEING AUTHENTIC

Living in the Now

If the only time you have is now, then choosing how you live now is vitally important. You can't change your future; you can only change now. The way to get to a future where you are living authentically is to be that authentic self right here and now. There's a famous quote that says this well:

> "The way to get there is to be there."

You can't pre-book authenticity. The only way to achieve it is to live it moment by moment. Obviously, this isn't something you can achieve at one time and then have forever, like winning an Olympic gold medal. It's something that unfolds, over time, throughout your life. For most of us in the Western world, this is a very weird idea, and one that is quite uncomfortable. We've been so heavily conditioned to live anywhere but now.

The media is full of sad stories of people apparently trapped by their past - victims of abuse, of tragedy, of disaster. There's a whole branch of the legal profession making a lot of money by claiming compensation for these sad pasts.

Now, I am not denying that some people may need or deserve some compensation for what has happened to them. Yet you only have to watch reality TV to see that, for many people, their sad story can easily slide into becoming their identity, their reason for living. They don't want to let go of it because then who would they be? Nobody special. An ordinary person.

On the other hand, self-help literature is future-focused. Yes, your life now may be utterly grim and horrible. Up until now you may have been a total loser, an utter failure, a nonentity. But next year? 10 years from now? You could be a millionaire! You could have the good life! You could be a success! Just focus on where you want to be and head for it.....you've probably read a dozen books like this.

But living now - who would want to focus on that? There's nothing happening! There's nothing here! Yet here is where the real "Rich Life" happens. The Self you came to this planet to be is here now. He or she could never _not_ be here. The life you came to this planet hoping to have is unfolding now. It's here - it can't be anywhere else. There's nowhere else for it to be.

-- --

The real heights and breadth of that life may still be in seed-form - but it's a seed that is here, now, in you. It's not out there. It's not in the future. It's here. Right now, you have no past to escape from or release and you have no future to grow into. In this moment, all that you are is here. The way to have that wonderful life, the deepest dream of your heart is to find it inside of you now and to put your focus onto that seed-self.

No matter how small and insubstantial that self seems now compared to the great multi-coloured dream you have on your vision-board, it's totally real, right now. Where else will your vision grow from? How will you ever become the Self that you need to be in order to be doing and having all the things that you dream of?

You have to be living as that Self, now. You can't become an oak-tree by starting growing as a carrot. And you can't become that greatest, most authentic version of yourself by starting growing as a fantasy, a dream, an imaginary thing.

Remember, authenticity is not an identity you have to create for yourself. It's not like being a celebrity and developing your image to match your media strategy.

Your authentic presence is the sum total of all the moments you have spent really being yourself, grounded, focused, centred, aware and Real. Does that sound rather boring? Actually, nothing could be further from the truth!

The "Rich Life"

Think of a happy memory - sometime in the past that you still look back on as one of those completely golden days. It may be a walk along the beach, realising that this was it- you had really met the right person, and you were so in love. Or the day your first child was born. Or that wonderful creative period when it seemed that brilliance flowed through you and you did your very best work ever.

How alive did you feel then? How much joy did you feel? What were you seeing, hearing, smelling? You can probably remember it all with unusual clarity. Times like that seem to get recorded in 3-D, with extra vivid colours, with surround-sound and special effects - the memories are so clear. Now tell me, at that time, how much were you focusing on your past? Or on the wonderful future you intended to create someday? My guess? Not at all!

That's what life is like when you focus in the Now. You've probably experienced it as a child playing, when you totally lost track of time and the day seemed to go on forever. If you're fortunate, you'll have experienced it as an adult - perhaps when making love, or having a fantastic holiday. If you're extremely fortunate, you may even work like this most days. But for most adults, this state happens rarely.

How is it that children live in a world of intense sensations, glowing colours and timeless days, whereas for many adults, many days just whiz past in a grey, stress-filled blur? It turns out that children have very different brain-waves from adults.

I don't know how much you know about brain-waves, but they get sorted into groups by frequency - basically, by how fast they vibrate. Most adults spend most of their lives having <u>beta</u> brainwaves - brainwaves that vibrate between 14-24 cycles per second. Children below the age of about 7 spend most of their lives having <u>theta</u> brainwaves - much slower brainwaves between about 4-8 cycles per second. The point is that adults generally experience theta brainwaves only when dreaming, when meditating quite deeply, experiencing "flow" states or when in a hypnotic trance.

Theta brainwaves enable us to heal deeply, integrate new experiences, or create deep-level change. In theta we become much more aware of the world - colours seem much brighter, music touches our heart, smells are more intense. Time stretches out. We have space between our thoughts in which to get insight or inspiration. We can learn easily and quickly; this is the state Zen Buddhism calls "beginner's mind" in which we don't automatically judge and reject new information and experiences.

This is the world we access through meditation and mindfulness. We see what is really there, instead of what we expect. We experience the Divine in the silence behind the noise. We're able to release fear and experience deep joy and gratitude for the beauty all around. Maybe this is what the Bible was referring to, when it says that only people who become like small children get to experience the Kingdom of Heaven?

So the missing link to experience "The Rich Life" is to be 100% here, where life is actually happening, instead of lost in our dreams and internal dialogue.

When we are caught up in the busy fast-moving world of beta brainwaves, there is so little space between our thoughts that not only do we miss a great deal of what is happening around us, we fail to see the opportunities to become a greater version of ourselves. Travelling at that speed, we don't spot them - they pass us by in the blur. We only see the habitual, straight ahead road, and so we rush blindly on into an endless repetition of more of the same.

The more you practice mindful awareness, the richer your life becomes. Most importantly, you start to open up gaps in the endless stream of your thoughts, allowing you to notice the choices in each moment, and so start choosing a more Real life.

What's my Real Self like?

How can you tell whether you're being Real or not? How do you recognise your Real Self?

We're so used to living a life made up of ideas and stories that the thought of just simply living can seem terrifying. Who would I be if I let go of all my stories about who I am? Who am I if I release my past and detach from my dreams of the future? You may be able to feel yourself scrabbling for something to hold onto.

You're perhaps OK with the idea of letting go of the grey, speed-blurred version of your everyday self for a better story about who you are, but what's the new story?

Is this like a religious conversion experience, when you feel "born-again?" Is it like an enlightenment experience (at least as depicted in the media!) where you can suddenly perform miracles and know all kinds of things you didn't know ten minutes ago? No. It's simply letting go of all the stories and noticing what is <u>actually</u> there. Who are you already? The great fear is that what is there will turn out to be nothing, or nothing much. Or that the answer to "Who am I already?" will be "Nobody."

When you first start to meditate, it can feel as if you're turning off a soap-opera filled with angst and action to do nothing more exciting than look out of the window. But slowly, as the dust of your thoughts starts to settle, you realise that you are not built like a tornado - lots of angry noise and motion swirling round an empty centre.

Inside you, there's a solid resting-place. There's a Real person in there. There's you, the real you, sitting in calm and quiet, minus the stories, just fully, vibrantly <u>here</u>.

If you'd like to listen to a guided meditation that helps you align with that still centre, you can listen to one here: http://chirb.it/J4y0Cb
Or, if you prefer quiet meditation, you can try this:

KINDNESS MEDITATION

1. Think of someone you really love - someone who makes you feel all soft and warm, just thinking about them.

2. Hold that person in your awareness, and imagine waves of love pouring towards them from your heart. Sit until you can feel this strongly. (You can stop here if you haven't got much time.)

3. Now bring to mind someone about whom you are fairly neutral - a work colleague, perhaps, or a neighbour.

4. Hold that person in your awareness, just as you did for the previous one, and imagine waves of love pouring towards them from your heart. Again, sit until you feel this strongly. (If you want to stop now, you can.)

5. Now bring to mind someone with whom you have been having problems. It could be a recent problem or an old one from way back.

6. Hold that person in your awareness, just as you did for the previous one, and imagine waves of love pouring towards them from your heart. Again, sit until you feel this strongly. This may bring up a lot of emotion, but breathe through it, and keep pouring out love. If this is a big hurt from your past , you may not feel much love first time, but just do the best you can.

7. Now hold yourself in your awareness, as if you were looking at someone else.

8. Let love pour from your heart to you. (Some people find this bit hardest of all.)

This is not an easy meditation for many people - but the effects can be far-reaching.. You can let go of old pain that has been hurting for years, and experience finally forgiving someone and letting them go. Take it at your own pace and go easy on yourself, especially if your past has some difficult stuff in it. If you really feel ready to let go and heal, this can help.

Over months and years of meditating, you discover your Real Self almost by a process of subtraction - the fake falls away.

You let go of your past, one chunk at a time. You may not even be aware that you've done so, until one day something happens to you that always used to press your "hot button" - triggering rage, violent weeping, withdrawn sulking, dark depression or whatever. Only this time you don't react. You may be aware of a "blip" of discomfort, embarrassment or upset, but then it's gone. You suddenly realise that you're free. You've released something, finally forgiven someone, simply stopped.

Your attachment to your vision board future falls away, too. You drive past that mansion and realise that honestly, you couldn't care less about having a house like that. The great pull of desire has just disappeared.

You suddenly realise it's been months since you thought about being promoted to the corner office. In fact, you're thinking of leaving your job altogether and working somewhere smaller and friendlier. You're thinking of working fewer hours and seeing more of your family, rather than getting that beachside home in Barbados. You begin to intuit that, somehow, on a deep level, these things have never mattered all that much to you - not compared with time spent with your kids, with your family, out in Nature, time spent being creative, or giving yourself some space to relax and heal.

Something interesting happens the more and more you start practising being simply here, intending to be the clearest, most loving, most creative and most peaceful version of yourself. Once you stop chasing it so hard, the "Rich Life" starts to turn up around you. When you commit to being who you really are, the person you came to this life to be, the life of your deepest heart's desire seems to happen almost by itself.

You start meeting interesting people who connect you to other people, work opportunities, new ideas, new books and new websites. You read one of the books that sparks a new interest that takes you in a new direction. You attend a talk someone told you about and meet someone there who changes your life. A new work venture opens up that maybe initially doesn't seem to have anything to do with the direction you thought you wanted to go in, but just feels so right. After a few weeks or months, it opens up a whole new doorway.

When you have choices to make, which one to choose becomes obvious in the moment. When you are centred in your Real self, you make congruent choices that take you deeper into Reality, rather than pulling you out. You're more connected to intuition and can feel which choice is right.

You're likely to have much more of a sense of being guided. You may have meaningful dreams or a series of "interesting coincidences" such as finding a white feather every time you think about one of your choices.

Most obviously of all, your life starts to feel more and more "on purpose" in a way it didn't do before. You know you're on track. This is not to say that everything becomes totally straight forward, because it won't! As Deepak Chopra says, some things in life seem to happen just to "thicken the plot!" There's a quote you may have come across:

> "The only time Success comes before Work is in a dictionary!"

There's a strand of thought in some self-help books that, if you're doing everything right, you can learn everything you need through joy, instead of pain. This idea has obviously come about to counter-balance the idea held throughout much of history that learning could <u>only</u> happen through pain. According to this idea, children wouldn't naturally learn unless they were beaten, the best way to make criminals reform was to flog them and the way to make heretics repent was to burn them at the stake. We've moved on, and I'm glad!

Yet you only have to talk to enough people to realise how much people do learn and grow through pain.

You see stories in the press and on TV about people who say things like, "It sounds weird but Cancer was the best thing that ever happened to me. I rethought my whole life during those long months and I understood for the first time which things in life were really important."

Sometimes, suffering and pain seem to bring out the best in people. So you hear about parents who lose children to congenital syndromes and who then put enormous energy into fundraising for the research that means other parents will not have to go through the same pain. Or people who are able to forgive their child's murderer and to pray for him or her with genuine compassion.

However, valuable as they might be, there's no need to seek out difficult times in order to learn and grow! Let's look at some of the difficulties that are likely to arise on the path - with no help at all from us!

CHAPTER 11: THINGS THAT GO BUMP ON THE PATH

Surely, the path is blissful?

Many New Age books seem to suggest that, if you're doing it right, living a spiritual life will be almost wall-to-wall joy and bliss. All the material things you want will manifest around you. Angels will turn up with tow-trucks when you break down. God will act like a well-oiled vending machine in the sky and answer every one of your prayers. Meditation will be a daily experience of releasing stress and opening to love and peace. In short, everything ever afterwards will be wonderful. Well, guess what? It's not like that.

Of course wonderful experiences will happen - but so will a whole bunch of not-so-wonderful things. This is Real life - not Disneyland! When difficult things happen, it doesn't mean you're doing your spiritual practice wrong. It may be a potent sign that you're doing it very well. Something is happening. You're clearing out the attics and the basement of your mind - odd stuff is likely to turn up. When you're Spring cleaning, you don't freak out if you find some dust, cobwebs or spiders - that's why you're Spring cleaning!

And even if you find something totally yucky - mouldy food, a wasps' nest, something that has been leaking for months - you don't take that as evidence you are doing this all wrong. It's evidence that you made a good choice in deciding to Spring clean before this problem got even worse. It's the same on the spiritual path. So let's take a look at some of the things that may turn up.

Self-Doubt
There's no "maybe" about it - self-doubt <u>will</u> turn up. You'll wake up one morning and suddenly, the very idea that you even <u>have</u> an Authentic Self seems ridiculous, let alone the notion of seeking to become it, to embody it in your life. You'll begin to wonder how you could have been taken in like this.

You'll have days when that little "Oh, yeah?" voice in your head is going nuts, having a non-stop rant. " Who are you to think there's anything special about you, anyway? What makes you think that you could be different from everyone else in your family? And what on earth made you think that meditating every day was going to change anything?

Even if you think meditation makes a difference to some people - it's obvious that it's not going to work on you - you're too old/young /stupid / crazy/(fill in the gap)." Tell it to shut up and go away. If it sulks, smile nicely at it, give it 10 out of 10 for a truly inspired rant and <u>then</u> tell it to shut up and go away. Remember the quote:

> "You don't have to believe what you think!"

Self-doubt happens to everybody. It even happens to people who don't think they are on any kind of spiritual path at all - so stopping now won't get rid of it, anyway. Just recognise that this is a self-doubt attack and not a sudden profound insight into an unsuspected truth. You're just having a difficult 10 minutes or so.

This is normal. Do something to shift your mood as quickly as possible. Put on some crazy music and dance like a maniac. Walk round your home, roaring like a lion - it's surprisingly effective at getting rid of negative emotions and making you feel on top of things again. Read something inspiring. Go and run round the block. Chant a mantra like YES! YES! YES! for 10 minutes until you feel fantastic. If you don't know how to chant mantras, the instructions are coming up.

MANTRA MEDITATION

This is what most TV soaps etc think of as meditation -they have characters sitting cross-legged chanting OM,OM,OM. But your Mantra doesn't have to be OM (Christians can meditate on "Jesus" or "Grace", for example)- and you don't need to say it out loud, either. So you can meditate on public transport without worrying that you'll get locked up!

Basically, a Mantra is a word you focus on. It doesn't have to be Sanskrit - anything you find positive or inspiring will do. In fact YES makes a good mantra. So, here are the instructions for Mantra meditation:

1. This is a meditation you can do while you're moving about if you choose to. So rather than sitting down, you may want to combine it with walking or running. However, you can sit, lie or kneel if you'd rather.

2. You can close your eyes or leave them open - your choice. (Obviously, leave them open if you're moving about!)

3. Focus on your chosen word - silently, chanted, or spoken. You can also sing or shout your mantra - a good way to change your emotional state if you're feeling slightly crazy.

It often works well to tie it in with your breathing , so you repeat your mantra the same number of times with each breath.

4. If you find your concentration drifting, don't beat yourself up- just focus again on the mantra.

5. If you're a beginner, aim for 2-5minutes. As you get more experienced, you can increase to as much as an hour, if you like. (In small steps - don't jump from 5 minutes to 1 hour!)

The main thing to bear in mind with self-doubt is that it's just self-doubt and that it will wear off by itself. However, it will go away a whole lot more quickly if you refuse to pander to it, and take vigorous steps to get into a more positive frame of mind.

You have no time to meditate

We live in a culture which believes that more is better. More fun. More music. A bigger TV screen. More special effects. Crisps with more crunch. More distractions. The idea that you might feel better with less is difficult for many people. Having a mobile phone means that your friends, family and clients can get hold of you 24 hours a day, 7 days a week. Having a laptop or tablet means that you can bring even more of your work home with you.

It can be difficult to find the time to meditate , reflect, read inspirational books, go for a quiet walk or even just to relax and do nothing. There's always one more email, one more call, a good film on TV, a comment to reply to on Facebook or a Tweet that you just have to re-tweet to your circle....and somehow, the time for meditation evaporates, disappears.

Here's a thought that can help. Missing out the messy decimals, 15 minutes is 1% of your day. Make a commitment to yourself that 99% of you is enough for your friends, family and boss. They can live without your input for 1% of the time. Make a commitment to take 1% of every day - without fail - for yourself. For your sanity. For your wellbeing. For your soul.

Use that time as you see fit - meditate, reflect, get inspired, relax. But spend that time every day doing something that brings you deeper into Reality and more in touch with yourself. It may be the most important decision you ever make.

Changes in your Health
It sometimes happens that as you continue to meditate over weeks and months and years, you notice that your body seems to be responding differently.

For example, you may find that there are particular foods which you have been eating for years that are now making you feel unwell or uncomfortable when you eat them. Or alternatively, you may find yourself wanting to eat foods that have not previously featured in your diet. You may even crave them.

Lifetime steak-eaters suddenly find they feel better on a vegetarian diet - or even a vegan one! People who have been vegetarians for years start craving fish or meat. You may find yourself wanting to eat less sugar, less dairy food or fewer artificial additives.

This isn't planned, but simply because you start to notice that some foods fog your brain, make you more paranoid or anxious or lower your energy. Similarly you may find yourself wanting more greens, fruit, fish or brown rice, simply because you realise it makes you feel so good. You may also find that some foods and drinks start to affect your focus in meditation. For example, many meditators eventually find that they need to reduce or eliminate caffeine.

Tune into your body and be prepared to let go of the rule-book - whichever rule-book you've been holding onto. Obviously, get yourself checked out by a doctor if you feel worried, but it's very common for meditation to do this.

Difficult Emotions - Anger, Jealousy, Irritation, Grief, Sadness

In our society we often grow up lacking skills in handling difficult emotions. Most of us were brought up to fear them and to avoid them if at all possible. So we take tranquillizers. We get drunk. We take recreational drugs. We comfort eat. We do anything so as not to feel our anger, our disappointment, our sadness, our grief.

Consequently, difficult emotions are often stored away in our bodies, locked up in our cellular memories. Meditation can free these up, often totally unexpectedly. So you can be sitting in meditation, feeling pretty calm and peaceful and then find yourself in floods of tears for no apparent good reason at all. Or feeling furiously angry. Or else a memory can arise - apparently from nowhere - of something from your past that you haven't thought about in years.

You are not going mad. This is not the beginning of a breakdown. It's simply a sign that the cleansing and healing aspects of meditation are working on you to release something from your past. Don't resist the emotion. Let it happen, and then let it go. The healing work of meditation is done and you are now free forever of that little packet of pain.

Impatience

The Western world has become addicted to the idea of instant gratification. No money? Don't save up, slap it on your credit card! Don't know how to do something? Don't worry - there's an amazing course that will teach you 20 year's worth of work by using specially tailored brainwaves and hypnosis - in a weekend!

The snag with devoting your life to the spiritual path is that it takes - well - a lifetime. Despite some of the ridiculous advertisements you sometimes come across in New Age magazines, you cannot become enlightened overnight - or even on a seven-day course! There's a wonderful quote from Warren Buffet that expresses this well:

> "No matter how great the talent or the effort, some things take time - You can't produce a baby in one month by getting nine women pregnant."

There are definitely times when you'll get bored and irritated with the whole thing. This may especially be the case when you have been releasing lots of difficult emotions.

It can also happen when life seems to be showing you where you are still a bit stuck by repeatedly putting you in situations that set off your "hot buttons."

Be gentle with yourself! You don't have to be a fully-fledged saint by next week. Here's a meditation that can help. I was taught it by two friends of mine who learnt it from Osho.

LAUGHING MEDITATION

Most of us believe that something 'out there' has to make us laugh, but actually, you can make yourself laugh - genuine, deep belly-laughs - whenever you want. This meditation is even funnier if you do it with other people - you can end up with a roomful of people all laughing hysterically!

1. It helps if you loosen yourself up physically first. So bend and stretch and shake any tension out of your arms and legs. Move about as you do this meditation, or stand still, whichever feels best.

2. Now start to make laughing noises, quite slowly at first. So you start saying out loud - HA! ...HA!.... HA! ...HA-HA! HA-HA! ... HA-HA! ... HA-HA!... HA-HA-HA! .... HA-HA-HA!

3. At first, you'll feel totally stupid or utterly fake but keep going. In a minute or two, real laughter will take over - you won't be able to stop it! You'll find yourself genuinely laughing.

4. Keep going as long as you can - some people can keep this up for 10 minutes or so. It releases all kinds of beneficial chemicals in your body and totally changes your mood very quickly!

Changing tastes

Just as your tastes in food can change, so can your tastes in other things - including which friends you enjoy spending time with. You may find you make a whole lot of new friends in a short space of time. These will usually be people who share your growing spiritual focus. At the same time, you may find yourself seeing much less of some of your old friends. It can start to feel that you just don't have so much in common as you used to.

You may find you don't enjoy the same old activities in the same way - your tastes in films, music and TV may change. Some people notice this much more than others; it doesn't necessarily happen to everyone. But don't be surprised if you find that it's happening to you.

Spiritual Greed

This is a tricky one because at first it can feel like a good thing and it may take you a while to recognise it as a kind of trap.

You have an amazing experience in meditation one time and you want to get it back. So you try hard to make the meditation head in that direction. When it doesn't - and it usually won't - then you feel a sense of disappointment. You start judging your experiences. "Well, it was an OK meditation today, but definitely not as good as the one last Thursday," or whatever.

You read a spiritual book that tells you about some guru who could walk on water or levitate or manifest flowers out of thin air. You think how cool it would be to be able to do things like this. How come your meditation doesn't give you abilities like that? Maybe it means you're not really very far along the spiritual path at all? Maybe you're no good at this. Perhaps you're doing the wrong kind of meditation.

This is spiritual greed - sometimes called spiritual materialism. You're trying to "get stuff" through your spiritual practice.

Instead of being here with whatever is really happening now, you start to imagine a future where more exciting things are happening - mystical insights, psychic gifts, deep realisations.

Before you know where you are, you're not here and now at all, but somewhere else in your head. It's difficult to spot that this kind of thinking is not on a higher level than fretting about the gas bill - but it's not! Reality is here, now. Keep coming back to it.

Weird/Psychic Experiences

This does occasionally happen to some people, but is by no means universal. You've been meditating for a while and then one day you realise you can see auras, nature spirits or your departed relatives. You start to have hunches about stuff that's going to happen or prophetic dreams. You seem to be sensing information about people that you couldn't logically know.

Don't worry. This is an occasional side effect of meditation and it doesn't mean anything. Quite often, the psychic abilities subsequently disappear. Alternatively, you may have them for keeps; you'll find you integrate them and get used to them and they fade in importance.

Most people I've come across who've found that meditation released psychic gifts in them came from families where such things were definitely not unknown, and perhaps even commonplace - so it may be a genetic thing to do with how your brain is wired.

Loneliness/ Lack of Support

It does help to have support on the spiritual path. So what do you do if you can't find any kindred spirits on a similar wavelength? If there really don't seem to be any local groups you are drawn to, it's worth looking online. There's a fair amount of dross out there, but also some excellent groups. The great advantage of online groups, of course, is that the other members can live on the other side of the planet from you. These days, distance is not so much of a problem.

However, one of the interesting things that can happen as you practise is meeting in your own neighbourhood the kinds of people you would have been prepared to swear did not exist there only a few months ago! It's fascinating to see how people can turn up in your life, completely unexpectedly.

They may not look like your expectations, but the most unlikely people can be working in local shops, waiting tables at local cafes, waiting by the school gates, or running local businesses. Be prepared for surprises!

The longer you are on this journey, the more you come to see that life is on your side. The next chapter explores this idea of life being a co-conspirator with you.

CHAPTER 12: LIFE AS A CO-CONSPIRATOR

Could it be true?
I first came across the idea of life as a co-conspirator in Deepak Chopra's program, Synchro-Destiny. I thought straight away that it was a wonderful idea, but at the time it simply wasn't a (conscious) reality for me. Now, it's obvious - an everyday lived experience.

So what does it mean, to have life as a co-conspirator? Well, one meaning is that - no matter what appears to be happening on the outside - life is always on your side, always working to bring you closer to your heart's desire. I know that it very often doesn't look like that. Difficult and tragic things happen. Sometimes we go through "bad patches" that seem to last for years. It's very hard to believe that any of this could be bringing us closer to what we truly want - or anything even remotely close to it.

The Olympic Vision
Yet just imagine that, in the time before you were born, in the life-planning space between lives, you had become completely fired up with the vision of becoming an Olympic athlete.

You decided you would win a medal at the Games - preferably a Gold one. You would have discussed it with your guides and perhaps even had guidance from angels to check that this was a good goal for you. Perhaps you'd have realised that the qualities of intense determination and perseverance you would have to develop would be a permanent gain for your Soul-Self, consolidating character qualities in yourself that were presently somewhat underdeveloped. Whatever the reasons, you decided to go for it.

Perhaps you then chose to be born in a family where both parents were keen on fitness and were amateur sports players of some skill. You'd perhaps already agreed with the soul who would become your coach, that they would "discover" you at a teen athletics competition and nurture your talent. All the help you needed would have been put in place. Of course, once you were born, you'd have no conscious memory of any of this at all!
  Now fast forward 17 years........

It's 5.30 am on a cold November morning, and black as pitch. A bitter wind is bringing in sleet, blowing almost horizontally, so it stings your face. Because, of course, you're out in this on yet another training run.

Beside you, your coach is running like a mad thing, screaming encouragement, advice and exhortations to run faster. You can't hear most of what he's saying, because the wind whips away his words. At this moment, you think you probably hate him more than you've ever hated anyone.

How come, you ask yourself, you had the bad luck to be born into a family of utter fitness fanatics who have somehow talked you into this? How come you're running through horizontal sleet while your mates are all tucked up in bed, sleeping for another couple of hours? And how come you'll be out again on Wednesday morning, doing it all over again?

To your teenage self, life at that moment may well seem like Hell. If some great and wise soul were to turn up saying such things as "Wonderful! I'm so glad to see you working so hard on the deepest desire of your heart," you may well feel inspired to punch them.
"What?" you'd say, "The deepest desire of my heart? Mister, you are SO wrong. At this moment, the deepest desire of my heart is a bed with a hot-water bottle in it, followed by three more hours sleep, followed by a hearty breakfast of porridge slathered in Golden Syrup.

I don't know where you got the idea that my deepest desire involved being frozen to the bone and shouted at by this lunatic here, but you are quite wrong."

Of course, three years later as you stand on that podium while an Olympic judge fastens a gold medal around your neck, and the crowds are cheering ecstatically as the band tunes up to play the National Anthem, you are happier than you've ever been before in your life. This is more than just a medal. For you, it feels as if it was meant - as if you were destined to be here, somehow. And of course, you were, but you'd never have got here without those 5am runs through the sleet. Even though at the time, the runs through the sleet were dreadful, they arrived in your life precisely to help you fulfil your destiny, your soul-purpose.

Can you see that a similar dynamic may have been taking place in your life at various times? Your goals for this life may not have been as concrete as an Olympic Gold - they may have been to develop new levels of compassion in yourself, to help relieve animal suffering or to learn a deeper trust.

If you look back over all of the difficult things that have happened in your life from the viewpoint that life is <u>always</u> on your side, what were the hidden gains, the deeper opportunities they offered you? In what ways are you a different person because of what has happened to you?

Some doors may have closed forever - and it's easy to get stuck focusing on them - but which doors have opened? What potential in you is now awakened, that might otherwise have slept forever? What are you now free to be, do or have that might never have crossed your path otherwise?

If you imagined that everyone and everything in your life was co-operating with you to help you learn and grow in the ways you chose to do before you were born, how could that change the way you look at life? If your Higher Self thought it was worthwhile for you to go through all the things you've experienced, what do you think it saw as the positive gain you'd receive in return? Remember, your life isn't chosen for you by some evil deity who is setting out to punish you for something you did 20 lifetimes ago. Neither is this all some test of faith - like some kind of Reality TV show with eternal bliss as the prize for the winners, while the losers get to go home with empty pockets.

<u>You</u> chose this. And you almost certainly weren't intending for it all to turn out tragically. In the space between lifetimes, when you could see more clearly what the benefits would be and you had all the help you needed to make wise decisions, you clearly saw that there was a good chance that you'd pull this off. You truly believed you could do it. <u>You</u> believed in yourself.

You saw that - through all that happened - there was a way you could rise to the occasion and bring out the very best in yourself. You weren't under any illusions about how hard it would be, but you truly believed you could make it. And you believed the rewards would be worth it. We have probably all used the excuse before now: "Well, I'm only human - what do they expect?" But, truth to tell, every human being contains the seeds of unexpected greatness within them. There is more to each of us than meets the eye.

Sleeping Beauty - so nearly a tragedy
Remember, no story is a tragedy until the end; it could turn into a story of a last-minute success against all the odds or a true hero's quest. Think back to the fairy-story of Sleeping Beauty.

Remember the Prince, who rides up to the impenetrable forest of briars that have grown around the enchanted castle. The only way in is to start slashing down the briars with his sword.

If he'd known beforehand that this bit was going to be in his story, he'd have turned up with flame-throwers, heavy equipment, chain saws - at least an electric hedge-trimmer! But no, in the story, he only has a sword. It must have taken him hours - maybe even days. (Fairy stories tend to skip over the dull bits!) Don't you think that there may have been moments when he was tempted to give up? Would there not have been times when he thought "Oh, blow this! If one more rose thorn tears one more bit of skin off the back of my hands, I'm going to pack it all in and go home?"

And if he had done so, that particular story would have become a tragedy. The Prince and the Princess would never have met. He may well have lived a loveless life, always looking for the girl of his dreams. She may well have slept forever, or at least until centuries later when someone turned up with heavy plant to knock down the forest and the castle, and construct a motorway there. The whole story would have gone wrong.

Of course, we know what did happen - and they all lived happily ever after. But at those points when it would have been so easy to give up, the Prince didn't know the end of the story. As far as he knew, it could so easily have turned out to be a tragedy - the sad story of the Prince who was led astray by some stupid old wives' tale and came home bleeding all over, with his clothing in tatters and his fine sword all blunted, defeated by a magical forest.

You don't know how your story will end. In fact, there could be a number of different endings, depending on the choices you make now. So how can you choose the course of action that leads to the best possible ending? Firstly, it's important to trust that there <u>can be</u> a good ending. It may not be the ending your personality self would most want, but there is always an ending available that takes you closer to your soul-purpose for this life. There's always a course of action that brings out more of who you are at your best, your deepest self.

> " I know God will not give me anything I can't handle.
> I just wish that He didn't trust me so much."
> Mother Teresa.

One of the keys to coping with hard times is to stay present. If you imagine the weeks and months ahead - more of this stress, more grief, more sadness, more pain - difficult times quickly become overwhelming. Yet moment by moment, you have the strength to cope. The difficulty is less in what is happening to you, awful as it may be, so much as it is in the stories your mind is spinning about it all.

Use every technique you find helpful to stay in the here and now and to focus on your breath or on what you are doing rather than the dramatic monologue running through your head. Eventually, all bad times come to an end. Maybe it is only in retrospect that we fully see the good that comes in their wake - the gift at the heart of the challenge.

Finding your greatest good
If at a deep level time and space don't really exist, and all of Creation is right here and now, then somewhere in what's here and now - even in the bad times - is your greatest good. It can't be anywhere else, because only here and now is Real. So somehow, right here, right now, is the perfect place for you to be - you wouldn't be here otherwise. The more you meditate, the more you discover how to find the still centre within you from which the answers arise.

When you rest in that still, clear space, the right action to take often becomes obvious. In fact, you'll often find yourself taking it without even thinking about it.

At times when the right thing to do isn't obvious, you can ask for guidance - which can come in very unmistakable ways! I remember walking past a bookshelf in the library and having a book literally fall out and land at my feet. And of course, it turned out to contain just the information I was looking for. I have heard of people who saw the answers to their questions written on billboards, or spelled out in the number plate of the car driving in front of them. Other people turn on the radio, only to hear the answer in the words of a song or being discussed in an interview. Neale Donald Walsch, writer of the "Conversations with God" books famously got the answers to his questions dictated to him by an internal voice as he wrote.

Learn to trust that life is on your side. This sounds simple, but it isn't easy because in the Western world, the prevailing paradigm people live by includes the belief that life is fundamentally against us and we can never stop fighting.

So we fight terrorism, fight crime and wage war on disease, strive to "win the inch war" against our waistlines, fight to get 'our' candidate elected, defend our families against germs, wage war on want and fight to preserve natural beauty spots. I never realised the extent to which I had spent my whole life burdened with fear about the bad things that could happen - until I lost it. I'd never noticed until then how much I believed that at its heart, life was out to get me.

What happened then was another deep meditation in which I <u>saw</u> the love that is behind Creation. Buddhists talk about "Basic Goodness" being the underlying Reality of life. I had heard the words, but thought that they were just that - words. I thought "Basic Goodness" was a nice, religious phrase that was using woolly, imprecise language to talk about things that we might not otherwise have labels for.

The meditation experience showed me that life really <u>is</u> basically good - in fact, we are all afloat in an ocean of goodness. There is more goodness around us than we ever see, miracles happening every minute, an amazingly rich and beautiful experience unfolding moment by moment to which we are largely oblivious. Not only is there more goodness and beauty around us than we see, but there is <u>more</u> than we could even imagine.

Basic Goodness is Reality - it's huge, infinite. We can't even fit a king-sized duvet into our heads, so our chances of beholding the immensity of Basic Goodness are pretty poor!

WHAT ARE YOU BEING OFFERED NOW?

We miss so much. A useful practice is to take the question "What am I being offered now?" and to hold it in the back of your mind all day. Come back to it whenever you remember it. Sit with it as a meditation focus for five or ten minutes from time to time - and see how your experience of life opens up.

I was amazed the first time I tried this. I see myself as quite an aware person and consider myself to be already quite grateful for the good things in my life, but this took my practice to a whole new level. I really came to see over a day or two how much is being poured out to me by an utterly abundant Universe and the only limitation is how much I am open to receive.

I know so many people on spiritual paths who are devoted to doing good in the world - they work as healers, servers, helpers, teachers, carers of all kinds. But so many of them will say that they feel they give too much. They feel that they give much more than they receive.

Consequently, it's hard for them not to burn out. It's difficult not to end up feeling resentful, used, worn out, stressed and fed up. A commonly given solution in books about spiritual business is simply to charge much more for their services but this isn't always possible - or desirable. If you know anyone like this, please share this practice with them because it can transform lives.

Once we start to become aware of how much is being offered to us in each moment - how much love, kindness, gratitude, beauty, wonder, joy and grace is all around us - the pendulum starts to swing the other way. We start to see ourselves as living a rich life in an abundant world. We start to perceive ourselves as deeply loved and cared for. We begin to feel that we have riches for the giving and that we can afford to be generous.

When difficult things happen, the simple question "What am I being offered now?" can open up enough space for us to see the choice in the moment. We have the opportunity to see the good intent behind this, the hidden gift in the present. Taking just a moment to ask the question can save us from our habitual responses that trap us in Victim mode and unresourceful feelings of self-pity.

We have a second to reconsider, to centre ourselves, to find the still haven of sanity and peace within. Suddenly, the freedom is there to choose differently, to choose to be a greater version of ourselves.

This is not some heroic and Puritanical operation about keeping a stiff upper lip and holding fast to the path of virtue, like some character in "The Pilgrim's Progress." This is about living a life filled with genuine joy and gratitude. It's about living a truly rich life.

In fact, the longer you do it, the more your life starts to feel like a love-affair with God. On the one hand, there is the Universe, constantly pouring out good things into your life. On the other hand, there is you, who now aware of this from moment to moment and lives in such a state of gratitude that you are constantly open to new ways to give back, to share your Gift and to help others.

What do you think is the result of feeling that you have so much to give that you are actively seeking for people to share it all with? You attract into your life more love, more gratitude, more compliments, more wealth of all kinds. And what do you think is the result of that?

You become ever more grateful and perceive your life as even more abundant - so you look to share even more of your Gift with even more people. The cycle builds and builds.

It's as if you've spent your whole life up until now on the shores of the Ocean of Abundance, walking mostly in dry sand, with the occasional foray into the very edges of the water. Now, all of a sudden, you are striding out into the waves, laughing in exultation as the water washes over you, splashing your friends and generally having the time of your life.

It sounds too simple that such a big shift can come about from being mindful in each moment, especially of what you are being offered. It's one of the traps of the drama-queen aspect of our personality-self to make the spiritual path into something mysterious and glamorous as well as incredibly difficult. It's easy to be persuaded that there are deep secrets to be had, weird mantras and esoteric symbols that will unlock Enlightenment for you - for a suitable fee, of course.

But the truth is to be found in each moment by quite simply being present there and seeing the wonder and beauty in everything else that is there with you.

We <u>want</u> the spiritual path to be complicated because that gives us the perfect excuse for not getting involved - "Too weird, man!"
 "All that woo-woo stuff, I can't get my head around it."
But the truth is so simple, it's accessible by children. It's accessible by anybody who can stop charging ahead just for the moment it takes to be truly still and to smell the roses. They smell heavenly! Take some time today to appreciate the natural world - smell the flowers, listen to the birds or the wind, and watch the play of colours in the sky. You live in such a rich world.

CHAPTER 13: LIVING IN THE NOW

How do you do it?
If the key to being truly present lies in becoming more mindful, how do you do it? I've already discussed how meditation can help with this. Let's take a look at other ways you can increase your own mindfulness.

Developing mindfulness isn't quick - it will probably take months or even years to develop real expertise. But you'll notice a definite improvement in a few weeks. Even a small increase in focus and awareness produces a big gain in how you feel. It only takes a few weeks of sustained practice before you start to notice that you feel calmer, more alert, and less easily upset. You're starting to spot more of the delightful details that make life so rich - the flower growing through a crack in the pavement, the smile on a stranger's face, the birds singing behind the sound of the traffic or the appetising smell from the bakery in the supermarket.

Becoming more aware of your body
Unfortunately, our culture is very "neck-up." Some people seem barely conscious of having a body at all, except as a convenient transporter for their head.

We eat on the run, or sitting in front of the TV, barely noticing the tastes and textures of the food. The clock-watching way of life that starts in school continues throughout our adult life, so we tend to eat breakfast, lunch and dinner at "the usual" times, whether or not we are even hungry. Many of us repeatedly eat the same one dozen or two dozen foods, instead of the three hundred or so different foods that our Stone Age ancestors probably ate.

When we feel ill, or are in pain, we tend to use medication to blank out our body's signals to us, so that we can continue the clock-driven routine of our days. If our body persists in giving us messages of distress, we go to a doctor and either get stronger medication, or get the complaining part removed surgically.

On the other hand, we want our bodies to look good. So we spend hours in the gym, running on treadmills and rowing on machines, rather than being outside climbing hills in the fresh air or rowing on real rivers, feeling the wind in our hair and the rain or the sun on our skin. For many people, 'fitness' is more about being in control and fighting their body than it is about getting more in touch with it and taking a delight in how it feels. You can do it differently.

It's possible to relate to your body in a more meditative, aware and reflective way. Try a class in Tai Chi or Yoga. Explore one of the body awareness programs that help you notice how you move, such as Alexander Technique or Feldenkrais. Take a dance class that encourages you to use your body in new ways - maybe belly dancing or a class in Gabrielle Roth's Five Rhythms. Take up a martial art. Or simply start a daily program of stretching exercises or regular gentle walks.

Tune in to your body before meals and notice whether or not you are truly hungry. What kinds of foods does your body really want to be eating? You may always have a cheese roll for lunch, but would your body prefer some warm soup right now? Or a fruit salad? What do you feel about an omelette, or a piece of fish? We do all have, buried inside us, the same instincts for what to eat as healthy animals have.

Babies are very clear, and will spit out food when they've eaten enough, or if this isn't what they want to be eating. However, after years of being fed when we're not hungry, and of eating foods that baffle our inbuilt satiation indicators - chocolate, caffeine, sugar, artificial flavours and the empty calories of processed foods all snarl up our instinctive responses - we lose touch with our innate body wisdom.

The good news is that we can rediscover it. Eating a wide range of natural foods, and cutting out artificial substances helps us tune in once more to our natural mechanisms that tell us what we need to eat to maintain health. Our bodies are wonderfully equipped to keep us well when we pay attention to their signals.

Notice when your body wants to move. The human body is not well adapted to sitting almost motionless in front of a TV screen, a computer, or behind the wheel of a car - as so many of us do. Notice when you are getting uncomfortable and stop and walk about. Stretch your legs. Drink some water. Have a few deep breaths. You'll be amazed at how refreshed you feel when you get back to what you were doing.

The more you get used to noticing your body, the more aware you will become generally. You'll start to find yourself more present, more of the time - and that's where the magic of the rich life truly happens!

Becoming more aware of your thinking

Until I started meditating, I was hardly ever aware of thinking as a stream of thoughts that I was letting run through my head. I was like a fish that doesn't know what water is, because it's in water all of the time.

I was never out of thinking. I had rarely experienced being deeply present without a constant running commentary. And when that did happen, for instance when I was playing music or deeply engrossed in writing, embroidery or knitting, I didn't spot what it was I was doing that made these experiences so much more enjoyable than most things I did. I didn't register that it was being deeply present that made the difference.

Once you start to become aware of your own thinking <u>as thinking</u> your life changes forever and you make an enormous leap towards greater mindfulness. You wonder how it is that you can have had this non-stop monologue going on all of the time, and not have noticed. Even worse, you start to become aware of what utter rubbish most of it is.

We worry about things that will never happen and maybe could never happen. We have imaginary conversations and arguments with people we may never even have met. We re-run episodes from soap-operas and rehearse the dialogue from films. We recite advertisement jingles in our heads. (I hope you're recognising some of this!) We run endlessly through our "To-Do" list. We re-tell our sad stories about why life is unfair and we deserve special treatment.

Scientists have estimated that at least 80% of what most of us think every day is a repeat of yesterday's thoughts - and the day before, and the week before that!

Meditation finally gives you a break - some mental space between the drivel. You start to notice your own mind-talk - and that gives you the choice to disbelieve it. You don't have to believe everything you think, especially as many of the thoughts are not your own, anyway.

As you start to notice individual thoughts you'll become aware of this for yourself. You begin to be able to ask yourself, "Now, where did <u>that</u> idea come from?" Many of your ideas will be easily traceable - that idea came from your Mum, your Father believed that, Auntie Bessie was always saying that. However, there will always be some ideas that are utterly mysterious - you watch the thought pop up in your head and can only think, "Well, where on Earth did <u>that</u> come from?"

It's sometimes scary to realise how long you might have had some of these unhelpful thoughts and beliefs without noticing - and how much they've been undermining your self-worth, your peace of mind and your general wellbeing in the interim.

Another useful practice for becoming aware of your thoughts is to commit to keeping a journal and to working on it for perhaps 15 or 30 minutes each day. In your journal, you reflect on your day. You allow yourself the space to be honest about how you're really feeling. You get your crazy thoughts out of your head and on paper where you can look at them and start to reflect on whether or not there might be a better way of looking at your life.

It's useful to ask yourself sometimes, "What will this get me?" Going over and over all of your boss's wrongdoings in your mind may make you feel more justified in hating him or her and in feeling yourself to be a victim, but is that an outcome you want? Your boss may have genuinely done all of that stuff, but is the way you are thinking about it likely to cause a change in the near future? If not, what could you do instead? What outcome would you prefer? What choices do you have? Allowing yourself the space to think differently will create changes in what happens at work.

You can also start to take note of all the positive things that have happened every day. This builds a virtuous circle, because once you start to focus on positive things, you begin to notice many more of them.

The more wonderful little moments you spot, the easier it is for you to feel grateful and appreciative about your life. The more genuinely appreciative you feel about your life, the more good things come your way - simply because other people tend to enjoy working with and being around smiling, happy people who are appreciative and grateful.

Make a note of all your successes - the tiny everyday ones as well as the major milestones. Most of life happens one small step at a time, many of which we don't notice. Give yourself credit for small accomplishments - the biscuit you chose not to have, the 10 minutes you chose to spend reading to your child, the comment you didn't make to the person who was annoying you. Your brain is hard-wired to produce more of the behaviours you pay most attention to. So noticing what you do right is very much more productive than beating yourself up for what you did wrong!

Becoming more aware of your emotions

I used to think that my emotions were caused by events in the world outside and that therefore, I had no control over them. Other people "made" me get angry. Difficult events "made" me sad. I wanted to be happy, but no happy things were happening, so what could I do?

I now know that how I feel is my choice. I can choose to let go of annoyance, anger, resentment or judgment. Just because a thought goes through my head doesn't mean that I am obliged to run after it!

I can decide to release my sad stories. That's not to deny that these things did happen, rather it's saying that I've had enough of feeling like a victim. It's becoming aware that I have been using the stories as excuses to stop myself opening up to my full potential and to give myself a 50% life. I can draw a line in the sand at any point and decide that where I've been doesn't have to be where I'm headed. I can change. I'm not a tree - if I don't like where I'm standing, I can move. We all can.

Of course, it's not that simple. We always have a choice but over time, our sad stories become part of our identity. Without them, who would we be? Perhaps someone who is just ordinary? Perhaps no-one special? We get attached to our sad feelings and hold onto them because they are our permanent excuse for living at half-mast. Nevertheless, from my own experience I have come to believe that all the difficult things that have happened to me were meant to act as a fuel to propel me forwards, not to act as anchors to hold me back.

In cutting the chains to the past and in choosing to release our sad feelings we gain tremendous power. We open the possibility to be the person we came here hoping to become.

By choosing to be present, here in the moment of now - fully present, really here - instead of living in the shadow of our own history, we uproot ourselves from our past. It will always be there, and it will always shape us, but we can start to choose how.

This planet is full of amazing people who have overcome every type of adversity. There are people who have experienced torture, rape and the death of people they loved and who have made a commitment to forgive. Of course, they didn't have to - the whole world would have understood if they spent the rest of their lives in bitterness and fear but they have chosen to grow instead of to shrink.

There are people who have learned to make the best of a life of enormous disability. If you ever feel sorry for yourself or just want to be inspired, put in "Nick Vujicic" as a search on Google and watch some of his videos. Here is a man born with no arms or legs, who has gone on to become a preacher working to restore hope to people who feel their life is hopeless.

You may not agree with his religious views, but you can't deny his brilliant success in turning round a life that would have made most people give up somewhere around square one.

The first time someone suggested to me that I could choose my emotions, I was shocked. Surely, that would mean my life was totally fake? Something sad would happen, but I'd be pretending to be happy? Surely it would be weird to respond to events and people "inappropriately"? Sad things were meant to make you sad, weren't they? Annoying things were meant to make you annoyed - wasn't that how things worked?

It took me a while to get my head around the idea that there were no "sad things", "annoying things" or "happy things" out there. There were just things, events and people. It was my choice to label them. It was my choice to decide that, now this had happened, I was supposed to get angry or I had to be upset. It was a shock to realise that I could make different choices.

What's more, I could let emotions flow through me without holding onto them. I could cry - and be immensely sad - and then let go of the feeling. I didn't have to keep on fetching it back all day.

I could be angry enough to roar out loud, or jump up and down, and then the anger would be gone. I could return to now - a now that didn't include anger. That anger was in the past and I had moved on.

It felt very odd the first time I dealt with a difficult emotional situation - a relationship break-up - by staying in the present. In the past I would have resisted feeling grief, because I would have been scared that the emotion would be too much for me to cope with. So I would have sat on it, pushed it down, tried not to feel it. Every now and again I might have cried, but rarely giving in to the emotion, so I'd spend a lot of time feeling dead and numb. I'd probably have felt shut down and depressed for weeks, or even months.

This time, with the encouragement of a friend who was training as a therapist, I stayed present with what I was feeling - and was astonished at the difference. Every now and again, I'd be hit with a wave of grief. I'd cry really bitterly, and would feel enormously sad, and then the feeling would be gone. A while later, I'd have another wave of grief. I'd never got over a relationship so quickly or so cleanly. It showed me that when I stay present in now, I can deal with whatever is happening - even when it's difficult. In the moment, it's tolerable, even if only just.

I realised I had scared myself in the past by imagining months of sorrow and building it into a big thing in my mind, which was then too scary to even look at. But we never have to deal with months of sorrow all at once. We only have to deal with the sorrow right now. And that is bearable.

I discovered that when I stopped shutting off uncomfortable emotions from fear of how awful they were going to be, I spent less and less time feeling dead and numb and more and more time feeling alive. I found that being unafraid to feel fear, or grief or anger or sadness seemed to take the lid off my ability to feel joy, gratitude, appreciation and happiness, too. <u>Now</u> can be filled with powerful emotions of all kinds - and our lives are richer for experiencing them.

Becoming more aware of Spirit

When I was a child, I was told about saints who had had visions, spoken to angels, heard the voice of God and who had experienced ecstasy - but it was very clear that such things didn't happen to normal people. These were special experiences, reserved for the chosen few.

Much to my surprise, I discovered later that these things are astonishingly common.

Something like two-thirds of Americans admitted in a survey that they had had at least one spiritual experience in their life.
There are now whole shelves of books in ordinary high-street bookshops about people who have met angels, had near-death experiences, visited Heaven, or seen visions.

Most people still don't talk about such things, though, because we all think it's only us. "Normal" people don't have stuff like this happening to them. Of course, to the people we label as "normal", it's <u>us</u> who are normal. They see us keeping quiet so they assume that normal people don't talk about such things - and so it continues!

So how do you get in touch with Spirit and then stay in touch? Here are some ideas:
- Meditation
- Prayer
- Inspirational reading
- Sacred dance
- Singing songs that help you feel connected (anything that works for you!)
- Listening to sacred music
- Walking in Nature
- Watching inspiring programmes on TV
- Having inspiring conversations

- Listening to CDs or DVDs of inspiring speakers
- Attending worship, either in person or online.
- Reflective writing
- Just taking a deep breath, relaxing, and coming back to your centre.
- Smiling - you can't smile and hold onto your sad stories and dramas at the same time!
- Feeling gratitude and appreciation for life
- Helping others - from regular community service to simply holding a door open for someone.
- Intending to put loving energy into whatever you are doing, whether that's cooking, typing, making music or driving.
- Sending loving thoughts to other people who are going through a difficult time.
- Creating beauty - whether that's making music, gardening, painting, arranging flowers - or whatever.
- Attending live events such as workshops and seminars for regular top-ups of inspiration.

Cultivate an awareness of living constantly in a spiritual world. We can all receive all the help and guidance we ask for. Ask and then have no doubt that that help and guidance will come. It might be an overheard snippet of conversation, a book, a TV program, a website - or even a song on the radio! If you ask for guidance, keep a look out for answers. Far from being hard to find, they are all around once you start looking.

CHAPTER 14: LIVING AT THE CROSSROADS

Making good choices

So here you are, at the crossroads. How do you make empowered choices? Even when you can recognise that choices exist and you have more than one option, how do you decide which path will lead you forwards to the best outcome?

Which paths will open you up to become a brighter and more expansive version of yourself and which paths will close you right down? Which paths will lead you to a future where you're expressing your Gifts and which to a lifetime of hiding your light? Which paths will lead to more joy, more gratitude and a greater depth of appreciation and which could leave you feeling mean-spirited, bitter and closed-off?

The secret turns out to be simple. The way to get there is to be there. The way to grow into an oak tree is to start from being an acorn, rather than a carrot. You can't step forwards into a future of shining your light from a present moment of lurking in the shadows, frantically hiding it. You have to step forwards from a space of shining - or at least of being willing and open to shine.

You can't step out into a future filled with gratitude and appreciation for the wonderful abundance in your life from a present in which you are terrified of lack and loss.

So how do you resolve the tension between living in the now and planning your life? How do you open to the inspiration of the moment while still respecting your responsibilities and paying your bills? How can you stay alert to unexpected inspiration and intuition while still making longer-term plans to take your life where you want it to go? How can you stay focused on your Big Picture while allowing yourself to be guided in the now?

How do you tune into the version of yourself that is most authentic so that you open up the most rewarding possible future? How do you uncover that Self that is shining, deeply connected to the world and everything in it, mindful in each moment of all the good things you are receiving and truly grateful?

You tune into it, moment by moment. You keep coming back to it, whenever you realise you've wandered away and lost touch with your centre. You begin to draw your rambling thoughts and scattered energies towards coherence.

Aligning with your Highest Self

I'd like to pull all these strands together now and look at some specific strategies for living at the crossroads - in that now-moment of decision making.

Here's a meditation that you may choose to do only occasionally, but that makes a very powerful daily practice. It helps you get a sense of what being your most Authentic Self feels like. By regularly practising it, you become able to tune in quite quickly when you are presented with a choice, so you can choose the option that feels most like your Authentic Self. In this way, you constantly take your life forwards in the direction of becoming and expressing more and more of the highest and clearest version of yourself that you can be.

MEDITATION TO ALIGN WITH YOUR HIGHEST SELF

1. Sit comfortably, and relax. Allow your breathing to settle and slow by itself - this may take a few minutes.

2. Draw together your scattered attention and bring your focus to your heart. Begin to breathe as if you were breathing in energy and love into your heart with each breath, and breathing out love to the world. Give

yourself some time to really get into this. You should start to notice a definite feeling of softening and warmth around your heart. Allow yourself to sink more and more deeply into the energy of love, until you can feel it strongly. This puts you on the Divine wavelength ensuring that you are connected to the high, loving parts of yourself.

3. Now begin to breathe that loving energy to every part of your body. Really feel Love flowing into every cell, healing and restoring you on a deep level.
Especially if you are at all unwell, this meditation is a powerful way to connect with the healing power of Divine energies and to open yourself to blessing, harmony and wellbeing. You can spend as long as you like on this part of the meditation.

4. Now breathe that Love energy through your thoughts and emotions, mentally intending that it clears away old patterns of responding that don't serve you. Rest in the feeling of tuning yourself to a higher level of harmony and coherence as your confusion and illusions are transformed.

5. Now breathe that Love energy into the core of your identity, mentally intending that

you become aligned with the highest, clearest version of yourself. Let go of any thoughts about what that might be like, and simply allow the Love energy to work on you, transforming you at the deepest levels. Sit as long as you feel comfortable, breathing in that immensely transformative energy and feeling it shifting and aligning you, centring you deeply in peace, light and love.

6. Breathe out that energy to your life, mentally intending that your life become aligned with your highest good, for the benefit of all creation. Again, let go of any ideas you may have of what that could look like and simply allow the love to do the work.

7. Enjoy the feeling of deep harmony and coherence that this meditation brings. Then, when you are ready, bring your attention back to the space you are in.

When I first started doing this meditation I set myself a 90-day challenge. I would sit and do this meditation every day and I would keep a journal to notice the changes I saw happening in myself and in my life.

It was an amazingly transformative time when my life changed very quickly. My work went in a whole new direction, my relationship deepened to a new level of loving and I began to meet groups of people who not only "got" where I was at, but wanted to work with me to get there themselves.(And pay me to help them!) I recommend you to try it for yourself; I don't know where it will take you, but I can be sure that it will bring you closer to living as your most Authentic Self.

The meditation works like a tuning fork - by holding yourself in a very powerful presence of the most loving and authentic level of yourself that you can access, you start to attune to that and to resonate more and more strongly with that frequency. As you soak yourself in that loving energy it's as if you begin to sing your soul-song at a higher octave. You are becoming a clearer and more harmonious version of who you are. What this does is to change the array of choices that are open to you in the moment.

New possibilities begin to emerge. All kinds of opportunities you may have never imagined begin to cross your path. People turn up in your life who have just the skills and information you need to help you move forward.

You discover books and websites that somehow you had always overlooked in the past, but which are full of inspiration and guidance. You also notice that all kinds of things are no longer happening. People who totally wound you up before are no longer affecting you - or they disappear from your life. Situations that regularly pushed your "hot buttons" now produce no more than a wry smile from you.
You experience more and more gratitude as you perceive more and more goodness in your life.

This is a very different approach from using the Law of Attraction to get a shopping-list of "toys". Instead, you are accepting that you may not consciously know what your greatest good looks like, but you are trusting enough in each moment in the Basic Goodness underlying everything to allow yourself to be guided towards it.

You need to know that if you have any lingering beliefs in a punitive God-in-the-Sky -with-a-score-chart, this practice will probably bring them to the surface!

It can feel very scary to trust this deeply. It can be confronting and threatening to our sense of wanting to be in control to <u>not</u> make 5-year plans and bullet-pointed "To-Do" lists.

I simply suggest that you experiment. Take it as slowly as you like - it's not a contest. Allow yourself the time to relax into it. I spent years changing from the plans-and-lists approach to life to this practice of Deep Trust. But even small steps towards opening to trust will enormously enrich your life.

Seeking the Vision

Many Native cultures from Native Americans to Australian First People encouraged their young people to seek a Vision for their lives. We in the West have lost touch with the need for a Vision, but it's there in our psyches, as strongly as it was for our ancestors. As the Bible says:

> "Where there is no revelation, people's lives unravel;
> but blessed is the one who listens to wisdom's instruction."

This is often translated as "Where there is no Vision, the people perish, but happy is he who keeps the law," but the modern translation more accurately carries the sense of the original words.

It's important to realise that this quote is not talking about vision in the "vision-board", Law-of-Attraction sense.

This is not about me having a clear picture in my head of the exact BMW that I want to have. This is about me getting a Vision with a capital V - a revelation of the life that is my Soul-work or life-Purpose - and then following up on that Vision by living in accordance with it.

In my childhood, I would have believed that only saints and others who were Divinely chosen in some way merited Visions. Now it is my belief that we are <u>all</u> here on purpose, so every one of us is entitled to ask for guidance and insight as to what that purpose might be. This is not only in a once-in-a-lifetime way, but as ongoing help and guidance with the decisions of living. I truly believe that we can all have as much guidance as we ask for - but that once we've received it, it's then our responsibility to follow through.

The disadvantage of asking for guidance is that it completely removes any kind of excuse that we didn't really know what we should do!

So how do you seek for a Vision? There are lots of ways and you may develop your own process with time. But here is a method that I use frequently, that is based on the Visioning process taught by Michael Bernard Beckwith.

GETTING THE VISION MEDITATION

1. Be clear about the question you would like to be answered. What do you want some help with? Do you want a sense of your life purpose or do you just want to know what is the best next step for you over the next month/ towards being a better parent/ towards gaining more fulfilling work - or what?

2. Get into a centred and meditative state.

3. Focus on Unconditional Love until you are really feeling it. The aim is to attune yourself to the "Divine Wavelength" as much as possible and to feel deeply aligned with it.

4. In that open and aligned state, ask (however seems good to do this) "What is God's/Universe's Vision for my next step? What would be the best thing for me to do over the next 40 days to really move me forward in line with my life-purpose/towards being a better parent/towards gaining more fulfilling work/ fill in the blank?

5. Sit in openness until you get some feedback. This might be pictures in your head, words, the impression that it would be good to do x - whatever. You may want to write stuff down at this point - or not.

6. Now ask, "In order to do this in the best possible way, what do I need to become? How do I need to change?"

7. Again, sit in openness until you get some kind of reply/feedback.

8. The action focus you take away from this is not trying to make a plan to make your Vision happen. Instead, your focus is to change yourself - to become the version of yourself you need to be in order to live the Universe's Vision for your life. If you get everything out of the way in yourself that is not in accordance with that Vision, then the Vision will happen.

This is a meditation you may need to repeat to get results. You may want to do it every day for a number of days, until you become clear about your next steps. Don't worry if you don't get crystal clear pictures or a pin-sharp audio message telling you exactly what to do. Very few people do!

You're more likely to get a general impression, a few words, an image or two - or perhaps just a deep feeling of light and peace and a sense that your problem is being handled. Don't worry about it - in this game, I've found willingness counts for a lot.

If you're making the effort to open and wanting to align, the information can come through as dreams, you'll see something on the TV, people will make random remarks to you, or you'll read your answer somewhere- you'll get the message given to you somehow!

Again, this meditation can be very confronting because it takes away your illusion of being totally in control of your own life. It will bring up all your fears that Life/God is <u>not</u> on your side. What if you open to the Universe's Vision for your life and it's something awful?

What if it demands some great sacrifice from you, like insisting you go and work in the slums of Calcutta like Mother Teresa or that you give every penny you have to a charity for disabled children? The simple answer is that it won't - unless that is actually your own deepest heart's desire. And it will never <u>insist</u> you do anything. If you doubt the messages you get, do nothing. Wait and see what happens. If something is right for you, you'll tend to get the same message in several different ways.

Sometimes we scramble the signals we get, putting our own fears and beliefs in the place of true Vision. We tell ourselves what we expect to hear, rather than listen to the genuine revelations coming through from Higher levels.

If you seem to be getting strange results with this, make sure you take your meditation to a very quiet, still and loving place before opening to ask for the Universe's Vision for you. It's worth taking extra time to be in a deep state in which your mind is quiet and your internal monologue has stopped or is very much diminished.

The other thing that is worth trying is to enlist the help of a friend or two to meditate with you. If you all focus on one person at a time, and meditate for a Vision for them, then you will have several sources of input at once. Any Vision that you <u>all</u> tune into is likely to be genuine while weird one-offs can more readily be discounted. Genuine revelations will feel right and will feel loving.

We are so deeply loved. Despite the crazy distortions of some religious teachings throughout history, we all live in a deeply caring and nurturing world.

When we open to trust and allow ourselves to move forwards into our most Authentic Self, what happens for us is beyond our imaginings and beyond our dreams.
We truly have an unprecedented life - a life we couldn't have imagined before, because we had no concept that life could be like this.

Instead of a life full of toys and the symbols of success and happiness, we have the real thing - a rich life, filled with Love, Joy and Gratitude and the deep fulfilment that comes from becoming more of who we truly are, doing what we came here to do. Meditation takes us forward into a world with a still, solid centre. Our world becomes based on our most Authentic Self instead of being about trying to create an impression based on our ideas and beliefs about ourselves.

So meditation can help us to attune to the clearest and most loving parts of ourselves on a daily basis and can help us catch a Vision of the bigger picture for our life. But moment by moment, how do we decide what to do?

The good news is that you don't have to make a conscious decision about every tiny aspect of your life!

As I said earlier, a rose doesn't have to decide on the right order in which to open its petals. It simply has to be a rose, and let the unfolding happen. In the same way, when we are centred in stillness and love, any action we take will move us forward into authenticity - because it's coming from authenticity within us.

Over the months, as you meditate, you get more clarity about what it feels like when you are being clear, creative and loving - so it becomes easier and easier to move forward from that space.

But what about planning?
"That's all well and good," I can almost hear you say, "but I can't live all of my life depending on what I feel like in the moment. That's totally impractical! What about paying the bills? What about creating business plans? What about getting the cooking done, and the shopping, the cleaning and the ironing? What about sorting out schooling for my children and vaccinations for the cat? These are not all things that get done spontaneously."

Relax! I am not advocating that you relinquish all planning in your life! In the past, I was always a plan-down-to-the-last-detail type of person - and it worked well.

When I started University I had 3 children under the age of 8, lived 50 miles away from the nearest University, had no nearby parents to pick up child-care, a husband who worked irregular hours and had no handy reservoir of spare money to see me through. So meticulous planning in great detail was what I used to organise my life and, at the time, I couldn't have succeeded otherwise.

As I said, it took me years to get my life to the point where much of it gets decided in the moment and only a small percentage gets organised by means of long-term plans.
 And making decisions in the moment does not mean that I am now a total idiot, devoid of all common sense!

If I am in the middle of seeing a client, I may change my mind about what intervention to apply, based on my intuition and my sense of what is best in the moment, but I'm not likely to start shouting rubbish or to choose to run out of the room.

When I receive a bill, I am likely to decide in the moment to pay it now, or to put it by the computer so that I pay it next time I use Internet banking.

I'm not likely to choose to rip it up, fold it into an origami model or to stir my tea with it. So living in the now does not preclude living responsibly. Actually, we do all our planning in the moment, because there is no other time to do anything.

We also choose to change plans in the moment, based on current reality. The more able we are to adjust our plans in the moment, the faster we can learn from experience and the more easily we can benefit from intuitive hunches. However, making decisions in the moment does not prevent me from scheduling appointments - I simply use the current moment to write an appointment into my diary. When the day for the appointment arrives, I can choose to attend, or to make my excuses.

What it does alter is the 5-year plans I used to make for myself. I don't do the same kind of big-picture planning that I used to - planning years of my life at a time.

I believe that many of us have incarnated at this time to make a real difference to the world by bringing in a whole lot of new ideas, new ways of doing things, and new energies. Many of us are going to be doing (or are already doing) jobs that have never before existed, or working in ways that have never before been done.

We're navigating through unmarked trails, in a way that can feel very much like playing "Getting Warmer, Getting Cooler" with the Universe. We're tuned in to an inner system of navigation that seems to give us clear signals as to whether we're on the path or off it, but often with a very unclear idea of what our destination will look like.

For us, the whole left-brain, 5-year plan way of doing things can't work, because being open to intuition in the moment and allowing ourselves to respond to guidance seems to be an integral part of opening up to Divine energies and deeply trusting in them.

What I'm trying to do much more now is to be who I want to be, now - and allow my future to unfold from that. I've really taken on board that my point of power is now - this is when I'm alive and able to choose. If I keep choosing to be the clearest, most creative, most centred version of me I can find in each moment, what will open up from that is what Michael Bernard Beckwith calls "an unprecedented life" - which sounds and feels more alive and vital than a carefully planned life. I use my Visioning meditations to make outline plans, but leave much of the detail to the moment.

I no longer consider it appropriate to plan so far ahead in such detail as I used to. The plans always needed changing, anyway, as life is inherently not completely predictable! So the main result of spending whole days drafting them was that I had a greater sense of being in control of my own life. I felt a sense of security from imagining that I was now safe, because I had the future sewn up. Ha! Ha!

The plans quite often ended up making some part of my life enormously stressful as I battled to make my vision (little-v) happen against the total opposition of the rest of Creation, it sometimes seemed.

How often have you made a plan only to finally admit to yourself that despite trying a reasonable number of ways to make it work, life seemed to have other plans for you? And how often has it happened that you've just met someone amazing, or have been presented with an incredible opportunity, only to realise that the reason you are here, in the right place at the right time for this to happen is because several dozen previous plans all went (apparently) wrong? If your Master-Plan had worked to the second, you wouldn't be here at all!

Every time some major disaster happens - a plane crashes, a tsunami devastates a holiday resort or there's a train derailment - the press seem to find someone who was meant to be there except that they missed the bus, overslept, had a hunch not to go, woke up with gastric flu or whatever. Sometimes, the best thing that can happen to you is that your plan doesn't work out!
As Rumi said:

> "Don't grieve for what doesn't come. Some things that don't happen keep disasters from happening."

Since the beginning of this year, I've been increasingly making a spiritual practice out of feeling into what to do next and what to do after that with no plan other than to see where Trusting my Higher Self would take me.

My perception is that everything I've done previously seems to have taken me towards a life of my dreams, but very slowly. I'd like the process to speed up, so I've stopped offering resistance to letting myself be steered. What is opening out is certainly a life I'd not have imagined - running Abundance Programmes, doing Aura readings, writing, seeing clients for all kinds of things that I haven't advertised - I'd never have planned this. What I have is a rich life - and one I didn't expect.

If you are an ardent advocate of planning, all I would ask you is "How well is that working for you?" If the answer is "Fantastically - my life is fabulous!" then carry on writing plans.

You've doubtless come across the quote:

"If it ain't broke, don't fix it!"

However, if you feel, like me, that you could be moving faster towards the life of your dreams, try some cautious experimenting.

Try relaxing the planning for one or two areas of your life, and letting them unfold more intuitively and organically. Or try a 90-day challenge in which you practice Aligning with your Highest Self and Catching the Vision. Let go of all the planning for just 90-days and keep a journal to record what happens. You may be astonished at the changes!

CHAPTER 15: SOME FINAL THOUGHTS

Becoming "Metanoid"

Paranoia is, of course, the mental illness whose sufferers believe that other people are plotting against them and that mysterious forces are out to get them. Sufferers from paranoia are termed paranoid. I'd like to propose the term "metanoid" for people who believe that the whole world is part of a conspiracy to help them learn and grow and is deeply on their side. Whatever happens to them, metanoids trust that they will be given the resources to cope and that the outcome can be beneficial.

They believe - even if they haven't seen - that behind all of Creation lies Basic Goodness. They are increasingly coming to feel a part of everything else, instead of feeling cut off and separate. By becoming more mindful of what is really here and now instead of living in a fantasy world where their fears and doubts are constantly projected outwards onto an apparently relentlessly hostile world, metanoids come to perceive that life is incredibly rich and abundant and is endlessly presenting them with new opportunities.

Because they notice so much more than most people of all that life is offering to them in the course of every day, they are able to live from a space of generosity. Instead of operating from a space of perceived lack and insufficiency, metanoids see that Universal Abundance surrounds and flows through them as the ocean surrounds fishes. They can afford to give of their Gifts and to share the deepest levels of who they are because they know that on a deep level, giving and receiving are inter-linked.

It takes a determined effort, and a lot of energy to maintain the belief in a poverty-stricken world. You have to work very hard to resolutely exclude the good that is constantly being poured out to all of us. Metanoids find their lives becoming easier as they stop struggling to make the world fit in with their sad stories and instead just relax and perceive with gratitude and appreciation what is really here, now. This book is an invitation to you to become metanoid.

Your crossroads, now

I leave you as I found you, yet again standing at the crossroads - your crossroads. I trust that some of the ideas I've presented have struck a chord with you. I hope that you are now noticing more of your choices and are beginning to find more richness in your life.

Perhaps you have already started to see synchronicities and unlikely "coincidences" that start to happen more and more as you align with your Highest Self and the Universe's vision for your life. I truly hope that your meditation practice is beginning to open new doors for you, so that you are already beginning to know that you are more than you have believed until now.

Before you go, I want to tell you that I believe in you. I truly believe that it's no accident that you're reading this now. Whoever you are, you came to this world to make a difference. You have gifts that nobody else has in the exact same combinations. You can make a unique contribution to life. What's totally in your hands is how big you want that to be.

At every moment, life offers you choices. How much difference can you make? Which of the world's problems are you here to help solve? How much can you open up to let Divine energy work through you? How much joy, love and creativity can you allow into your life? How much abundance can you open to? Which version of You will you choose to become? The crossroads are before you. The choice is yours.

Made in the USA
Charleston, SC
08 September 2013